PATH TO

Freedom

LEADING A LIFE OF JOY, IMPACT AND ABUNDANCE

NADER VASSEGHI

BALBOA
PRESS
A DIVISION OF HAY HOUSE

Balboa Press books may be ordered through booksellers or by contacting:

Balboa Press
A Division of Hay House
1663 Liberty Drive
Bloomington, IN 47403
www.balboapress.com
1 (877) 407-4847

Printed in the United States of America.

ISBN: 978-1-5043-9087-3 (sc)
ISBN: 978-1-5043-9089-7 (hc)
ISBN: 978-1-5043-9088-0 (e)

Library of Congress Control Number: 2017916905

Balboa Press rev. date: 01/25/2019

CONTENTS

DEDICATION

This book is dedicated to my sons, Nima, Navid and Omid. Three beautiful and precious souls who have profoundly transformed my life with love, beauty and strength in ways that I could not have imagined. May this book help you on your journey of life to be all that you can be.

And, in memory of my parents, who showed me by example, how to live a life of integrity and compassion.

PREFACE

It all started when I stepped into the desert on a vision quest. At the time, I was in a career transition mode, trying to figure out what is next for me. I wanted to leave my corporate job and start a company that was more aligned with my passion. Naturally, feelings of uncertainty, doubt and temptations to stay within my comfort zone made me hesitate on taking the next bold step. So, I decided to go on a ten-day vision quest into the deserts of Nevada to clear my mind. The first three days were about working with the guides to learn how to protect myself in the desert. And then the solo quest started; heading into the desert with my sleeping bag and a few gallons of water. It was a big mind shift to be stripped away from any civilization or shelter. No one to talk to, no phones, no books, and nothing to do for four nights and five days. I had no idea how vulnerable, mysterious and magnificent it is to lay under the open night sky filled with an infinity of stars. The fourth night, called the vigil night, was the real test. I was to build a circle of rocks to represent my life, step into the circle upon sunset, remain awake and do not leave the circle until the dawn. The combination of cold, hunger and lack of sleep made it a very long and arduous night. After the long-awaited sunrise, when I started to head back to the base camp for integration, I was crystal clear that my path was to leave my corporate job and start my new company. And so, I did. The first few months was filled with passion, excitement and confidence except that the timing coincided with the economic meltdown of the late 2008. In spite of the financial pressures, I pulled together a great team, built a unique product and hit the market. And that is when the honeymoon ended. I was faced with major challenges and obstacles, internal and external, most of which were out of my control. I kept exercising my willpower, my determination, my commitment, but year after year, things got more difficult and I felt all the weight on my shoulders.

> *"The path of love seemed easy at first, but what came was many hardships."* —Hafiz

There came a point where my ego was shattered, my passion was washed away, and my will to fight was defeated. For a long time, I went into what Joseph Campbell calls "the abyss", a dark and lonely place where there are no lights at the end of the tunnel. After trying everything I could in an attempt to find a way out, I realized the only place to go was inside, and into my cocoon. Introspection, reflection, meditation and at times, depression took hold. I took refuge in reading books, going to quiet retreats and spending time with nature. I experimented with shamanic journey work as a powerful tool to access my inner wisdom and connect to my forgotten self. I immersed myself with music and the healing vibrations of sound. I got an urge to draw whatever caught my eyes - snapshots of the scenery at Esalen, flowers, animals, etc. I am no painter and have no formal training, but I toyed with the idea and got a lot of satisfaction out of it. It was a kind of meditation for me, a form of connecting with the object of my drawing. After several months of drawing various subjects of the outside world, I got an urge to focus inward and to capture and bring my inner visions onto paper. I went to the art store and bought myself a large white canvas and placed it on an easel in my work area. For several days I just stared at the blank canvas and wondered;

what wants to come out. Slowly, an image of a butterfly emerged. For me the butterfly has always been a symbol of metamorphosis. A slow crawling silk warm turning itself into a cocoon, and eventually transforming itself into a beautiful butterfly, flapping its wings away into a new dimension. I started to paint whatever ideas came to me; shapes, colors, symbols, mudras, etc. This process of inner creation took several weeks, and as soon as the painting was complete, words started to pour in. I began to write, primarily to capture my insights for my own reflections, but over time the framework and intention of the book revealed itself. Nine months later, this book was born with the original painting of the symbolic butterfly on its cover.

FRAMEWORK OF THE BOOK

Joy, impact, and abundance. These three words has been the guiding light in my life. In working with my clients, and in my own experience, I have discovered that to create a truly fulfilling life, all these three ingredients need to be present simultaneously. It is like a 3-legged stool where if one of the legs is weak or short, the structure is not stable. It is living inside the intersection of these three key dimensions that a life of flow and fulfillment is achieved.

For each of the three dimensions, there is an underlying character. The underlying character for joy is beauty. The underlying character for impact is strength, and the underlying character for abundance is love. Underlying characters are like roots of a tree. They are the energy source that feeds and nourishes the tree. The tree trunk and branches act as a bridgeway that navigates this energy source from the roots upward and turns them into its fruits. Joy, impact, and abundance are the fruits, the outward manifestations of the underlying characters.

This book is divided into four parts; each part focuses on a core topic: joy, impact, abundance, and freedom. Each part follows a consistent structure and is divided into three sections. The first section in each part sets the foundation and explains the core concepts and insights. The second section consists of a set of practical exercises and practices to help integrate the core concepts into your life. These correspond to the branches of the tree drawing upon the source energy of the roots (underlying characters of beauty, strength, and love) and turning them into outward manifestations of joy, impact, and abundance. The last section includes a set of tools and resources that can help you go deeper into the subjects.

My intention in writing this book was to make it as short, concise and practical as possible. This is not a book of information, it is about giving you the insights and tools for transformation. And transformation happens when you internalize the insights, and incorporate and integrate them into your everyday life. For this reason, doing the practices at the end of each core topic is essential to get you on your path to freedom.

Outward
Manifestations

Bridge
Practices

Underlying
Characters

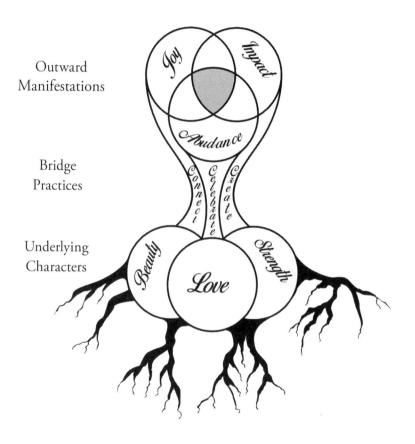

INTRODUCTION

This book is about the journey of transformation, thinking and living outside of the box, dreaming and creating the life that you were meant to live, and living to your full potential. It's about leading a life of joy, impact, and abundance. But what does this really mean? How do we actually walk on this path?

The first key ingredient is *awareness*. We must realize that every one of us tends to live inside our little boxes. We have created this box over time, starting in our childhood: right and wrong, proper and improper, good and bad, acceptable and unacceptable. Over time, we don't even realize we are inside these self-created boxes, and our views of the world have been limited, filtered, and shrunk.

The next key ingredient is *readiness*. Are you ready to make a paradigm shift, to break the bonds and fly away, to be transformed? Change is hard; transformation is much harder. Going outside of our comfy and safe boxes is not easy. We need to have a reason to do so, and we need to be ready for it. How do you think the caterpillar feels when he is going through its transformation into a butterfly? Is he going through confusion, loss of identity, worry, insecurity, and fear of the unknown? Or is he in complete trust and surrender to the process, allowing it to happen? Transformation requires allowing and surrendering to the process of becoming.

As humans, we go through two major transformations in our lives, no matter what. First, we come out of our mothers' wombs and into this world. The other is when we are passed on to another world upon death. In our lifetimes, many times we are invited to go through various levels of transformation consciously, but many of us decide not to answer the call and prefer to stay in our comfy boxes. Our egos have worked so hard to create safe and protective boxes around us, where everything makes sense. Why risk it?

Transformation requires awareness and readiness. It is a leap of faith. There needs to be a sense of connection to the self and to our personal powers. There needs to be trust in ourselves and in the universe—a divine power beyond what we see and are familiar with.

For the most part, this book contains reflections on my own journey of transformation. This journey was not easy or smooth for me. I had to face my fears, be lost in darkness many times, be knocked down over and over, and get back up again. During this journey, I learned a lot (although not quite willingly), and I was helped many times through seen and unseen forces. I witnessed the process of transformation taking shape, and I realized that there is no end to it. This is a journey of a lifetime.

I am writing this book in order to listen to my higher self, to transform myself into what I may be, to walk the talk, to dream myself into being. And to share my experiences and insights with you, so you may use them as guideposts and walk on this path with a bit more grace, awareness, and confidence.

> *"We teach best what we most need to learn." —Mike Dooley*

PART 1
JOY

The underlying character for joy is *beauty*. Invoking joy through the practice of *connection*. Joy is about connecting to our essence, to our authentic self, and to the world outside. To see the beauty within and without, and to be in the flow of who we are and who we are becoming.

What is joy? We start this conversation with the understanding that in the physical world, there are no absolutes. What joy means to you may be completely different than what another thinks. In this context, we need to move away from popular definitions and statistical norms. We are here to discover our own truths, and that needs to come from inside of us and not be subject to common definitions of right or wrong, good or bad, high or low, sacred or profane. Completely free and boundless. Completely real and based on our own experiences. And experience always happens in the present moment. What was joyful for us five years ago might not be quite as joyful today, and that is perfectly okay. Let's make sure we don't stick to our old definitions of joy. Let our joy be completely free, boundless, and timeless, like a river flowing through its course at each moment.

THE JOY IS INSIDE YOU

With that in mind, what does joy mean to you? What brings you joy? What makes you feel joyful? For me, it is sitting by the window, watching trees and clouds, listening to soothing music, and writing, as I am doing now. It is being by the ocean, feeling a flower or a butterfly, or feeling my own sensations in the hot baths of Esalen. It is watching my kids grow and seeing their smiles, excitement, hopes, and dreams. It is creating a work of art, turning confusion to clarity, and manifesting a vision to reality. It is mending a broken heart and reigniting a hopeless soul. It is creating intimacy with the other, where egos dissolve and boundaries vanish. It is appreciation of beauty in all its forms.

What takes our joy away? One of the main contributors is worry. Worry comes from fear, insecurity, and not meeting one's expectations. When there is worry, there is no place for joy. All the space is taken by worry and fear. But where does this joy come from in the first place, and how does it vanish all of a sudden? All these external situations that seem to create joy in us create a resonance to our own soul's vibration, so we can see and feel the magic in that moment.

> *"Everything is energy and that's all there is to it. Match the frequency of the reality you want and you cannot help but get that reality. It can be no other way. This is not philosophy. This is physics." —Albert Einstein*

Have you noticed that when we are in the state of fear or worry, the same, previously joyful situation does not invoke any joy in us? We are not resonating with that vibration; we are not feeling it. There is no space to allow and take in the magic of the moment. Our minds and bodies are preoccupied with worry and fear. We are carrying the old, heavy baggage of our past as we look at our uncertain and insecure future. But how can we clear ourselves of this fog? How can we free ourselves of this uninvited guest?

BE COMFORTABLE WITH THE UNCOMFORTABLE

> *"This being human is a guest house. Every morning is a new arrival. A joy, a depression, a meanness, some momentary awareness comes as an unexpected visitor … Welcome and entertain them all. Treat each guest honorably. The dark thought, the shame, the malice, meet them at the door laughing, and invite them in. Be grateful for whoever comes, because each has been sent as a guide from beyond." —Rumi*

We can do it by not running away. By observing, accepting, and realizing. By consciously getting ourselves out of this maze and wake up to our true state of being. By realizing that we cannot change the past, but we can change our perspective of it. We cannot avoid insecurity and fear, but we can learn to be friends with it, take in their guidance, and move forward through action. By realizing that worry is an unhealthy mental reaction to fear and insecurity, which depletes us of our energy and vitality. We always have a choice to make: we can accept the reality as it is, and then choose to either shift from the inside or change the outside to a place that feels better to us. Reinhold Niebuhr captured this beautifully in a prayer.

> *God, grant me the serenity to accept the things I cannot change,*
> *The courage to change the things I can,*
> *And the wisdom to know the difference.*

You may ask, "Is it possible to be in state of joy all the time?" I don't know, but I do know that we can increase the amount of time we enter and stay in joy. That does not mean we won't have any setbacks or challenges in our lives. Rather, we face them with courage and equanimity, and we operate from a state of internal strength and joy. By consciously taking ourselves or our minds away from worry and fear-generating situations, we create space and allow joy to sprout from within. We awaken the joy inside us.

One of the main reasons for losing our joy is losing the connection to our essence. We then start comparing, judging, doubting, and we lose our anchor, our sense of worth, and our direction. We feel lost, insecure, in need, and trapped in the land of fear and worry. We then seek approval and comfort, feeling a void that needs to be filled by external people or objects. Although this may feel uncomfortable, running away is not a solution. What irritates us often points us to aspects of ourselves that have come to surface for us to address.

Live from Your Essence

Let's explore ways we can connect to our essence. The first requisite is to stay curious about and open to our own experiences. We must see and appreciate the beauty that is in and around us. Beauty points us to our essence. When we don't see the magic in our lives, how can we see the essence of anything, let alone ourselves? Trust that there is a higher force—call it spirit, universe, divine, consciousness—and that we are not separate from it; we are always connected and guided by it. It resides in us, and we reside in it. The problem is not a lack of connection; it is lack of our awareness to the connection. It is ignoring and not trusting its presence.

I am not suggesting blind faith or a fake belief system. Our trust needs to be built on our personal experiences and observations. Not because it is written in scriptures, or even because it is scientifically proven. The only legitimate reason to believe is through observation and integration of our own experiences.

We are often so busy and entangled with life that we take things for granted and don't let our experiences touch our deepest core. We either become numb and foggy to our own experiences, or we are so rushed and determined to get from point A to point B that we miss the process and all the support we receive during the journey to get there. In either case, our experiences will not make any meaningful impressions on us and therefore do not reveal their teachings to us.

In order to help realize this connection, review your life and recall blissful moments when you experienced the universe's love and support, or when you were touched by beauty. You may have experienced this during the hardest challenges and darkest times of your life. You may have felt that despite the hardship, you were protected by a divine force. Or you may have experienced this through a spark of love with another person and felt in unity and harmony. Or it could be as simple as a quiet, serene walk in nature where you could sense the grace and presence of something beyond. Spend a few minutes to recall such experiences when you felt the presence of a divine force when you were touched by beauty. It is during these moments that we have a clear sense of a connection, a reflection of our essence back to us.

ALLOW AND FOLLOW

Once we get a sense of this connection, we then need to allow and follow. We need to get out of our minds and get into our hearts. We need to connect to our desires, aspirations, and dreams. We need to respect them, live them, and bring them forth. They are our guides and are the blueprints of our essence. Once we do that, we stop asking and start doing. We stop being a seeker and start being a giver. Asking continues to put us in the state of lack. Doing puts us in the flow. We will only find ourselves through doing, and doing can only happen in the now. Surrendering to this moment and responding wholeheartedly to what this moment is offering us without judgment or expectations. It's acting from our essence and offering our best selves to this moment. Such action is often effortless and natural because it comes from our essence, leading us to the state of joy.

Listen to your feelings, sensations, and aspirations. See where they are leading you. Sometimes they are asking you to step outside your comfort zone, to expand and explore. Sometimes they are asking you to take refuge, to incubate and wait. Sometimes they are asking you to go against the odds with courage and determination. The key is to respect and honor them. Listen, pay attention, and consider their guidance seriously. Most important, take action. You strengthen the connection to your essence by taking their guidance seriously, putting them to test, and acting on them.

Sometimes our instincts, intuitions, and gut feelings know in a more direct way. In our Western society, more often than not, we tend to ignore our intuitions and gut feelings in favor of logic and analysis. However, we must realize that they are not mutually exclusive. By utilizing both aspects of awareness, we will have a better grasp of the situation and a better chance of acting out of wisdom. Real-life situations often demand we make decisions based on incomplete information or even nonexistent data. This is where we can really leverage our intuition, which operates in a different realm and has access to information that our logical minds do not. You can think of it as whole brain thinking or alignment of heart and mind. Although this is a two-way communication pathway, the heart actually sends more signals to the brain than the brain sends to the heart. The nervous system within the heart enables it to learn, remember, and make decisions independent of the brain's cerebral cortex. There has been ample research on the heart-mind connection that suggests the heart-brain has a way of knowing without any reason or information.[1]

> *"Have the courage to follow your heart and intuition. They somehow already know what you truly want to become. Everything else is secondary."* —Steve Jobs

BE KIND TO YOURSELF

Sometimes we are more understanding and kind to others than to ourselves. We may feel it is a selfish act to indulge ourselves with joy, but with that mindset we are blocking joy from entering into our space. We need not only to allow but also to invite joy to come into our lives. One of the enemies of joy is our very own voice of judgment, the authoritative critique that is always downgrading, judging, and criticizing us. Simply be aware of this voice and choose to not react to it. You don't need to get tensed up about it; treat it as a frustrated kid who wants to be heard. You can bring it to your awareness, but let it pass. By bringing your awareness into the scene, you can emotionally distance yourself as an observer and not let yourself get into a reactive mode. Then there is judgment and criticism of others, not only verbally but also energetically. Know that people mostly project their own lack and sensitivities onto

---

[1] Rollin McCraty Ph.D., *Science of the Heart, Volume 2: Exploring the Role of the Heart in Human Performance* (HeartMath, 2015)

others. Be aware of this mechanism in others and, most important, in yourself.

> *"Everything that irritates us about others can lead us*
> *to an understanding of ourselves." —Carl Jung*

Learn to protect yourself against toxicities, both coming from outside as well as self-inflicted. When someone around you is grumpy, tense, or angry, the person might consciously or unconsciously want to release some of that energy onto you. Again, be aware of the situation and be compassionate, but realize and maintain your own boundary, and do not let energies that do not belong to you invade into your space. Maintain a neutral separation while showing understanding and compassion.

Take a few minutes and make yourself a joy list. Write down anything that comes to mind, big or small. Don't overanalyze, judge, or consider the how. Be as selfish as you want to be. Once you are done, review the list and pick a few that resonates with you and that you can take action over the next few days. Make a commitment to pick one joy activity each day during the next seven days. Observe your joy factor and see how taking simple conscious actions each day can shift your state of being toward joy. Nurture and feed yourself each day with joy, even if it is just for a few minutes. This is an especially effective way to move your mood to a more joyous state and make it a habit. The next time you feel down or tired, pick an item from you joy list and act on it. Experiment on yourself and experience the effects.

Another practice that can be even more powerful is to be the messenger of joy to another. We are wired to feel joy when we bring joy to another. Take a few minutes and make a list of what you think makes the people around you happy and joyful—family, friends, co-workers, and even strangers. Review the list and pick a few that you can take action over the next few days and commit to acting on them. Observe the effects on them and on yourself. A point of precaution here: view this exercise as random acts of kindness and have no expectations or attachments to outcomes. Be mindful to keep your ego out of it.

EXPRESS YOURSELF

When we are in our creative zones and are freely expressing ourselves, we feel joy and aliveness. This is natural because we are creative beings by design. When we open our channels of expression and creativity, we are allowing our genuine selves to come to life and present themselves. Unfortunately for most of us, this is one of the qualities that we lose early in our lives. Our families, peers, schools, and society overall, give us clear boundaries and definitions of what is acceptable and proper (often with good intentions). We are labeled, judged, scolded, and chastised as soon as we cross the line of what is considered the norm. Over time the creative child within decides to hide away and not risk it anymore. Our fire within slowly dims in order for us to be considered cool and accepted by the community.

However, our joy factor is directly proportional to the level of freedom in expressing who we really are. We can be meeting all the outward standards of success and comfort, but deep down something is missing because we are not living our true selves.

What are your natural channels of expression? They are activities that come to you effortlessly and give you joy. Maybe you have not given your creative child within the opportunity and permission to play and explore itself. In that case, it is time to play, stay curious, and experiment. Give yourself the freedom to try new things, to be bold and courageous, to make mistakes and be okay with it, and to bring out your gifts. It is only through action that we can discover what resonates with us, what wants to come out, and what channels of expression are most suited for us. The most difficult part of this journey is the initial few steps to overcome the inertia and habit, to open our minds to possibilities, to shift our state of mind and make the initial move. Once we start walking, the action itself draws us and nurtures us with more energy. We will talk more about this in part two of the book.

FACE YOUR FEARS

Fear is a natural emotion and is designed to protect us and our loved ones from danger. The obvious example is that it triggers our fight-or-flight response in the presence of a real threat. It serves a useful and fundamental purpose, and without it we would be extinct as a race long ago.

However, in this day and age, the problem is our fear mechanism is being constantly triggered based on trivial incidents, and mostly in reaction to imaginary threats. It is now a tool that the ego uses to protect itself.

We are stood up for an appointment, and our ego is hurt. In response we get frustrated and are ready to fight. Our opinions are not heard at work, we don't get the promotion we deserve, or we get fired. Our ego gets tensed up and wounded, and we are ready to break someone's neck. Our teenage kids ignore us, insult us, berate us, and make us feel powerless and helpless. Our ego is shattered, and we get furious and want to teach them a lesson they will not forget.

If only we could observe the situation from a distance and stay with the hurt, we would realize fight or flight is not the answer. Getting angry and accumulating tension does not serve us any good and will only aggravate the situation. We have lost the ability to instinctively release this pent-up tension and return to a state of relaxation quickly. Animals, after they get out of a life threatening or dangerous situation, literally "shake it off" and get back to living in the moment. It is like a reset button for their body and nervous system. Think about how a dog shakes, for no apparent reason, multiple times a day. Animals have it figured out!

Fortunately, we have not lost our instinctive ability to heal ourselves. Dr. David Berceli, during a long career of working with PTSD patients and people afflicted by war and disasters, developed a series of simple exercises (TRE)[2] designed to self-induce the natural human shaking process genetically encoded within us, allowing us to release the pent-up stress and trauma. For more information about these exercises please refer to "Tools and Resources" section of this chapter.

Then there are past fears and traumas that have been imprinted in our bodies and are looking for triggers to bring themselves back to life. We project, we judge, we criticize, and we prosecute. By doing so, we create our own stories to protect the ego from being broken again.

Today, most of our fears are ego based, not survival based. It does not serve any purpose other than giving us more pain and suffering. Instead of compassion and understanding, we get cruel and righteous. Instead of acceptance and allowing, we want to control and fight back. Instead of forgiveness and love, we are immersed in

---

[2] David Berceli MD., *Trauma Releasing Exercises* (BookSurge Publishing, 2005).

hatred and revenge. Instead of expansion and challenge, we get into contraction and withdrawal. The irony is that as long as we don't face our fears head-on, they become stronger and can completely run our lives, often without our notice. The only way to break this chain is to accept our fears and, in spite of their presence, walk through them and act out of wisdom. All it takes is a mindset shift and a willingness to act and experiment. Oftentimes we realize that by doing so, our fears suddenly fizzle out and don't have a hold on us anymore. Our fears are holding us back from what we can be. They are limiting us, numbing us, rationalizing us, and wasting our potential.

WHAT IS HOLDING YOU BACK?

When I was a child, I had a severe stuttering problem. In middle school and high school, my biggest fear was when my name would be called to recite a passage in front of class. There was no chance I could go further than a few words. I would get stuck at a word and could not move on, no matter how hard I tried. I felt awkward, embarrassed, and inadequate. During college, I avoided taking classes that required any kind of reading or recitation in front of others, so I bypassed the whole episode and almost forgot about the issue. But when I graduated and got my first job, I realized that I was required to speak in meetings and make presentations in front of others. Instead, all I could do was sit silently in meetings and accumulate frustration and fear.

I soon realized that if I was going to be successful by any measure, I must address this issue. I figured the only way to release myself from this fear was to face it head-on. I applied to teach a technology class at the UC Berkeley extension in the evenings. I was pretty good at technology and got accepted. I'll never forget the first day of class.

I was a twenty-two-year-old shy and timid boy, standing in front of forty students, most of whom were older than I was. Knowing my handicap, I had prepared myself and knew my material very well. But my problem was not about knowing; it was about bringing it out through words. The first session started, and it was then that I realized the situation I had put myself into. I had no way out of this and had nowhere to hide. The first session was a disaster. Fear took hold of me; I was red in the face and felt embarrassed, inadequate, and ashamed. I don't know how the session came to an end, but I remember that after the session, I was totally drained, wasted, and wanted to melt away and vanish from the face of this earth.

But at the same time, deep down I realized that the first session was over, and I was still here. From then on, it could only get better. And it did. The second session was also a struggle, but as I was going through the awkward motions, something inside told me that I would get over this. In each following session, I would get a bit more fluent and a bit more confident. Toward the end of the quarter, I was feeling pretty good about myself. I'd done it. It was over. But I wanted to make sure this plague was totally out of my system, so I decided to teach the same class again the next quarter. The second time around, it was a breeze. I knew my material and was able to communicate clearly and fluently. I was stutter free.

What is holding you back? What is your deepest fear that you may not dare to speak of but is running your life in the background? The fear that you know has limited your progress, but you have decided to ignore it? Is it fear of failure? Is it fear of not being accepted? Fear of being lonely? Fear of being found out as not authentic? Is it fear of not being loved? Spend a few minutes to reflect on what is holding you back from who you can be. Facing your fear is a choice. Make a decision to face your fears, to act in spite of fear. Courage is not lack of fear; it is acting in spite of fear.

PIVOT

Pivoting is a common practice in the world of business. The majority of successful start-up companies start with an idea, build the minimum viable product, and then go through many rounds of iterations based on customer feedback and market traction until they find the right mix. When the product does not quite show traction, they objectively consider the situation based on real data, and quickly reevaluate, and reposition the company or product. Oftentimes the resulting end product is completely different from the original concept.

There are many examples of this in the world of business. YouTube began as a video dating site called "Tune In Hook Up". Twitter started out as a podcasting platform. Pinterest began as a mobile shopping app called Tote.

Unfortunately, we hardly do pivoting in our personal lives. We tend to continue doing the same things that have not worked before, but we expect different results. We stay in a broken relationship, in an unfulfilled job, and in an unhappy state of being for months and years without making a pivot. Instead, we tend to ease our pain with remedies and distractions—alcohol, entertainment, side excursions and excitements—to cope with the negative situation, or we become numb and lifeless as a defensive, coping mechanism.

The negative emotions that we feel are signs and symptoms. They are making a statement that something is wrong here; otherwise, we would not be feeling these negative emotions. They are asking us for an evaluation and possibly a pivot. A pivot is designed to make a shift from a negative to a positive state. In a pivot, you must first observe, understand, and accept the current reality, and then have a clear idea of where you want to be. The moment you turn your attention to what you want, the negative attraction to negativity will stop, and the mental state is shifted to positive. You are ready to take action.

"Where attention goes, energy flows." —James Redfield

The key ingredient for a successful pivot is to have a clear idea of where you want to be. It is not necessary to know the details of how to get there, but your intention or desired outcome needs to be clear and specific. You need to be able to visualize the end result and be able to put yourself inside the picture.

FIND YOUR MAGNET

In his book *The Soul's Code*, James Hillman proposes that our calling in life is inborn and that it's our mission in life to realize its imperatives. He called it the acorn theory—the idea that our lives are formed by a particular image, just as the oak's destiny is contained in the tiny acorn. Joseph Campbell coined the term "follow your bliss" when it comes to discovering your calling.

> *"If you follow your bliss, you put yourself on a kind of track that has been there all the while, waiting for you, and the life that you ought to be living is the one you are living. Wherever you are—if you are following your bliss, you are enjoying that refreshment, that life within you, all the time." —Joseph Campbell*

Unfortunately, in a world full of distractions and outside influences, we often lose sight of our own calling and guiding mechanism, and we give away to what is most accepted, popular, or rewarded by the outside world. Over time, we become alienated to our deepest desires, and in spite of achieving outward success, we often feel empty and hungry inside. Luckily, the internal guiding light never dies. The feeling of dissatisfaction and emptiness is actually a healthy sign telling us that something is wrong, that there is misalignment and imbalance in our lives, and that we need to pay attention to it. This is actually part of our inherent, built-in guiding mechanism, which is unfailingly pointing us to our true north at all times just like a magnet, pulling us toward our souls' desires. Our present-moment feelings and emotions are always giving us clues and insights on what to do. We need to listen to them, pay attention, and take corrective courses of action.

> *"There's nothing capricious in nature, and the implanting of a desire indicates that its gratification is in the constitution of the creature that feels it. Our desires presage the capacities within us; they are harbingers of what we shall be able to accomplish."*
> —*Ralph Waldo Emerson*

The surest and fastest way to finding our magnet is through what I call *conscious actions*. It's *conscious* in the sense of being aware of the underlying drives, feelings, and emotions, using them as guides and pointers. Like a scientist observing his experiments with curiosity and openness, we can simply observe what works for us and what does not, what gives us energy and what drains us of energy. When we are on our path, there is a sense of joy and effortlessness.

It's *action* because without action, we can easily fall into our own (or other people's) stories, concepts and intellectual theories. It is only through personal action that knowledge can turn into wisdom. It is only through action that we are giving the universe a chance to respond to us with real feedback.

Each day we engage ourselves with a lot of unconscious actions that are autonomous and habitual. Over the course of the next week, give yourself the challenge to raise your awareness to your actions (as well as the actions from which you are running away). Ask yourself, "Why am I doing this? Why is this important to me? What drives me? Does this energize me or sap my energy?" If you realize that your action is not aligned with your heart's wisdom, then stop and change course. The idea is to be an essentialist. Sift through your actions and throw away the ones that are not essential, the ones that are not aligned with your essence. Bring present moment awareness and observe what resonates with you, what draws you. Feel the pull and align yourself toward your magnet. Replace random actions with the ones that are more meaningful and enjoyable to you.

Right Relationships

One of the most important ways we can discover ourselves is through our relationships. In a sense, we know ourselves through the other. We become real in relationship with the other. You can only call yourself kind, caring, and generous if you apply these qualities in your relationships. In a relationship, we recognize the other, and at the same time, we see ourselves in a mirror. Our relationships are always spiral acts of giving and receiving. The higher purpose of any relationship is to help each other heal and evolve. It gives us the opportunity to connect at the core and utilize this connection to nourish each other. This can only be possible if we can be authentic and true in our relationships. Oftentimes we store and carry a lot of anger, resentment, or hurt in our relationships with others, and yet we tend to push these emotional knots down and cover them up, not realizing or admitting the impact that they have on our bodies, minds, and souls, let alone our relationships. We have surrounded ourselves with many superficial relationships for so long that it often feels awkward and scary to have an authentic and honest conversation with the other. As a result, we rob ourselves and others of the opportunity to touch each other at the core, expand our boundaries, and experience joy and transformation with each other. Being authentic requires us to be true to ourselves, to be courageous and vulnerable. It is to listen with our hearts of compassion, and speak with courage and acceptance.

> *"Let's fly together in trust, otherwise we break the wings of our friendship." —Margot Bickel*

We are all faced with difficult relationships and are given opportunities to transform ourselves and others through these challenging interactions. We can withdraw and be the victim, the judge, or the prosecutor. Or we can open our hearts and minds to the experience and ask ourselves, "How can I use this encounter to heal and evolve myself and the other? What am I here to learn? What would the best version of me do in this situation? What would love do in this situation?"

One of the most important ingredients of transformation in a difficult relationship is forgiveness. Forgiveness is a choice that is based on compassion and wisdom. It is only when we can step outside of our ego boundaries that we will have the capacity and willingness to forgive. Forgiveness is like a detox remedy for ourselves and our relationship: it transforms the nature of the relationship at the instant of the act of forgiveness. It suddenly breaks the chains and frees us of our suffering and our tormenting stories. Like many things in our lives, we know intellectually that forgiveness is what is required, but we find ourselves resisting and don't quite know how to get over the hump. Forgiveness is not an intellectual conversation; it is a personal choice. It can only be experienced by action, by consciously walking past our ego resistance, being able to see ourselves in others, and jumping over the chasm with open hearts and minds. This is not a matter of how to, but a matter of want to. As soon as we make this choice, the world changes its grip on us, and the true colors of the relationship reveal themselves. That is when you know you have forgiven.

RELATIONSHIP WITH TIME

"Be here now." —Ram Das

This guidance has been given to us by many sages through the ages as the gateway to enlightenment. Living in the now means having the right relationship with time. Life can only be experienced in the present moment, but the quality of this experience is influenced by our relationship with the past and the future. Oftentimes we carry our regrets, hurts, and unfulfilled desires of the past into the present, and we mix them with the fears and uncertainties of the future. The result is a stew full of stress and anxiety that robs us from living in the now. Our perception gets tinted by the past and future, and we can no longer see the true colors of the current reality. The ability to live in the now requires us to observe reality as it is, without any expectations, wanting something that is not, or not wanting something that is. The minute we start craving for something that is not, or have an aversion to what is, we are no longer living in the now. Our minds and hearts get consumed by our own stories, and we can no longer take in the present moment experience. We lose our anchor and get off balanced, and our decisions become biased, subjective, and reactive.

> *"Calm and quiet mind, alert and attentive mind, balanced and equanimous mind."* —S. N. Goenka

Having a healthy relationship with the past means leveraging from the learning experiences of the past and bringing their wisdom to the present, without carrying the emotional charges and projections. Often this requires conscious acts of reflection and contemplation on past experiences in order to integrate the teachings into our lives. Unfortunately, what we do by default is just the opposite. We carry the emotional charges with us and let them dictate our reactions to the current reality. Therefore we keep repeating the same mistakes.

The story of one of my clients, Joe, illustrates this. Joe is a capable entrepreneur who loves to come up with ideas and build companies. He was starting his new company when I engaged with him as an executive coach. His previous company, which he'd started seven years back, did not make it, and he had to close it down after two years of operation due to lack of funding and lack of business traction. After a short discussion, I realized that he was still carrying a lot of fear and insecurity from his last start-up experience. Upon further investigation, I realized he was experiencing same issues and setbacks in his new start-up company, and the trajectory was pointing to the same place. Not only had he not learned from his previous mistakes, but he was carrying and projecting all the fears and wounds into the current reality. By doing so, he was putting himself in a state of constant insecurity and worry, which was draining his energy and limiting his actions.

Having a healthy relationship with the future involves planning ahead without any attachments to outcomes. The planning is more about helping you stay aligned to your purpose and focusing on your priorities rather than achieving a specific result. What we usually do, however, is to fixate on a specific outcome and then exert heroic control and willpower to achieve it. This is where we get into disappointment, frustration, and exhaustion because oftentimes the universe has other plans for us.

> *"If you want to make God laugh, tell him about your plans." —Woody Allen*

When you see the wisdom of the past and potential of the future in the present moment, that is conscious living. You can look at the present moment from two perspectives. One perspective is to see it as eternal, always here with no waiting or expecting for something else. Simply be with it and feel comfortable. The other perspective is to see it as a momentary gift. It is here now and will be gone soon, so take it in. Don't take it for granted, absorb it all, and live it fully while you can. Being in the here and now requires us to hold these two perspectives simultaneously and let life live through us.

DON'T TAKE YOURSELF SO SERIOUSLY

A fencing master used to say, "Hold the foil as if you were holding a bird: not too tight, otherwise the bird dies; not too loose, or the bird flies away." The same is true for our lives. Whenever you find yourself tensed up, stressed, and controlling, it is time to ease off and let go; you are killing the bird. Whenever you find yourself wandering and bored, the bird has flown away.

Don't get absorbed and tangled up in your own stories. The minute you catch yourself tensed up and tight, detach yourself from your stories, observe yourself from a distance, and ask yourself whether this is really important in the grand scheme of things. Sometimes when things go wrong, we need to be able to laugh at ourselves, knowing that this too shall pass. The parable of King Solomon says it well, when he teased his chief of army, Benaiah, with an impossible task of bringing him a ring with special powers that if a happy man looks at it, he becomes sad, and if a sad man looks at it, he becomes happy. After months of searching, Benaiah comes across a jeweler in the poorest parts of the city. When he inquires for such a ring, the jeweler gives him a simple ring with an engraving: "This too shall pass."

Sense of humor is a strong medicine for the body and mind. There is ample research on the therapeutic effects of laughter on health, from boosting the immune system, preventing cardiovascular issues, relieving stress and anxiety, and helping us live longer.[3]

There is even a practice called "laughter Yoga"[4], originally developed by a medical doctor from India, which is based on the concept that the body cannot differentiate between fake and real laughter. It is a series of simple exercise routines that is scientifically proven to reduce stress levels by 28% and lower blood pressure by 6%. To learn more about this practice check out the "Tools and Resources" section at the end of this chapter.

---

[3] Lesley Lyle, *Laugh Your Way to Happiness: The Science of Laughter for Total Well-Being* (Watkins Publishing, 2014)
[4] Kataria Maden, *Laughter Yoga: Daily laughter practices for health and happiness* (Ebury Press, 2018)

PRACTICE: CONNECT

The intention of this section is to bring you tools, techniques, and resources to help you *connect* to your essence and to the world outside, in a way of accessing and invoking a state of joy in yourself. It is the interplay of the world within and without that helps you sing your song and start your dance.

> *"We do not sing because we are happy. We are happy because we sing."* —William James

The only requirement on your part is to get engaged with the suggested exercises. If you want to get any value out of this section, you need to dig in, get yourself a pen and paper, and do the work. Simply reading and glancing through the exercises is not going to be enough.

Remembrance

Review your life and recall blissful moments of your life when you experienced a sense of awe, joy, and support. This could be witnessing the birth of your child, playing your favorite sport, or feeling intimacy and love with your partner. It could be as simple as walking in the woods and being touched by the beauty and serenity of nature. Close your eyes and recall whatever it was that touched your heart and soul.

_____

_____

_____

_____

_____

Joy List

Ask yourself, "How can I bring more joy into my life?" Write down whatever comes to mind, big or small, that brings you joy. Things to do, places to be, things to have, people to be with. Don't overanalyze, judge, or consider the how. Keep writing and make sure there are at least twenty items on your list.

_____

_____

_____

_____

_____

Review your list above, cross out the ones that do not invoke a sense of genuine joy in you, add ones that are missing, and underline the ones that really resonate with you at this time. Circle the ones that you can take action on over the next week. Make a commitment to pick one joy activity each day during the next seven days. Observe your joy factor and see how taking simple, conscious actions each day can shift your state of being.

_____

_____

_____

_____

_____

Expression

Explore your natural channels of expression, the activities that feel effortless and give you joy. This can be playing a musical instrument, writing, painting, dancing, communicating, using your hands to build something, gardening, and more. Maybe you have not given your creative child within the opportunity and permission to play for quite some time. Let your child free to explore itself. Make a list of whatever comes to mind that gives you a sense of expansion and expression. It is time to play, stay curious, and experiment. Circle up to three that you are committed to explore, nourish, and strengthen over the next few months. Take action.

_____

_____

_____

_____

_____

Magnet

What is your highest goal, your best version of yourself, your dream-come-true state? What drives you and excites you? What makes your heart sing? What is really important to you? Write down whatever comes to you. You need to be able to visualize the state and put yourself inside the picture. Review your list and create your vision statement.

_____

_____

_____

_____

_____

Alignment

Reflect on your major activities and actions last week. Draw a vertical line in the middle of the page. In the left column, write actions that were nonessential or misaligned to your magnet— actions that drained your energy. In the right column, write down actions that were meaningful and important to you—actions that gave you energy. The idea is to sift through your actions and throw away the ones that are not essential, the ones that are not aligned with your essence. How would you like this exercise to look like for next week? On the left column, cross out the ones that you'd rather not do. In the right column, circle the ones you'd like to do more of, and add ones you'd like to include.

_____   _____
_____   _____
_____   _____
_____   _____
_____   _____

Messenger of Joy

Make a list of what you think makes the people around you happy and joyful. Review the list and circle a few that you can take action on over the next week; commit to acting on them. Observe the effects on them and on yourself. View this exercise as random acts of kindness and have no expectations or attachments to outcomes. Be mindful to keep your ego out of it.

_____
_____
_____
_____
_____

Fears

What is holding you back? What are your deepest fears that you may not want to speak of but are running your life in the background? Is it fear of failure? Fear of not being accepted? Fear of being lonely? Fear of not being loved? Spend a few minutes to reflect on what has limited your progress from who you can be. Facing your fear is a choice. Make a decision to face your fears, and act in spite of fear.

_____

_____

_____

_____

_____

Relationships

What are the most difficult relationships in your life? What happens if you shift your perspective and view them as opportunities to transform yourself and others through these challenging interactions? Ask yourself, "How can I use this encounter to heal and evolve myself and the other? What am I here to learn? What would the best version of me do in this situation? What would love do?"

_____

_____

_____

_____

_____

Forgiveness

Is there someone in your life (current or in the past) whom you need to forgive? Or is there someone from whom you need forgiveness? Unresolved relationships are toxic for your well-being and block your energy flow. Write a letter to them from your heart of compassion and your mind of wisdom. You may or may not decide to share the letter with the person, but the act of writing alone has its healing effects.

_____

_____

_____

_____

_____

TOOLS AND RESOURCES

Meditation

Meditation can be a powerful tool to help quiet the mind so you can listen and connect to your essence. There are many forms and types of meditation, but they generally share the basic ingredients of focus (breath, object, mantra, sensation, etc.) and maintaining a state of nonjudgment and nonattachment to whatever that arises during the meditation. A state of mindfulness and equanimity helps us be grounded in present moment awareness. With ample research and reports on the multitude of benefits of meditation to health and wellness, it has gained more attention and has become more mainstream. However, with so many different types and schools of meditation, it might become confusing to choose the "best" one. Keep in mind that the best meditation is the meditation that works for you at this stage of your life. Some prefer intense sitting meditations like Vipassana or Zen meditation, some prefer walking meditations, and some prefer movement meditation like yoga or qigong. At the highest level, every action that is performed mindfully can turn into a meditation practice, even washing the dishes. Below are a few pointers and references for you to explore and see what works best for you. Whatever technique you choose, keep in mind that it needs to be practiced regularly and consistently. It might be hard to get it at the beginning, but if you keep at it and practice with patience, you will succeed.

- – Vipassana
- – Zen
- – Metta

- TM
- Yoga
- Self-inquiry
- Qigong
- Prayer

Guided Visualization

Guided imagery or visualization can be considered a form of meditation that comes with guidance and intention. It can accompany soothing or inspiring music to help achieve a state of calmness and openness. Imagination and visualization are often used to invoke and access hidden parts of the unconscious. Hypnotherapy (or self-hypnosis) techniques can be used to formulate and plant seeds of positive and empowering suggestions in the subconscious mind to be unfolded over time. Kelly Howell's guided meditations and Dr. Daniel Amen's medical hypnosis audio are good examples to look into.

Dream Work

Often invaluable wisdom and insight are revealed to us in our sleep through dream language. The key is to jot down our dreams as soon as we awake; otherwise, we have a tendency to easily forget them. We then need to learn and understand the language of our dreams so that we can interpret their symbols and meanings. Dr. Carl Jung's *Man and His Symbols* is a good introduction to understanding the world of dreams and the unconscious. Also, Robert Johnson's *Inner Work* is a great book on how to use dreams and active imagination for personal discovery and growth.

Shamanic Journey

A powerful tool to access wisdom beyond our egoic minds and gain deep insights into ourselves and the world is through shamanic journeying. This path has been practiced for ages by our tribal ancestors throughout history, from Native American communities to Australian aborigines to shamans of the Amazons and the Andes. There are many practices and techniques that are used to facilitate the access to the non-ordinary states of consciousness. These may include drumming, chanting, ecstatic dancing, breathwork, fasting, and in some cases the use of psychedelic plants and entheogenic substances. The idea in all of these techniques is to go "out" of your egoic mind, open your mind and heart to the mysteries of the unseen, and access and receive their wisdom and insights. In most cases, it is best to have an experienced guide, a shaman, who can hold the space and support you in your shamanic journey, as well as help you integrate the insights into your everyday life.

Journaling

Reflective journaling is a great way to capture your insights, thoughts, and emotions. The process of writing gives you the ability to be an observer to your own experiences and helps you raise the level of your awareness to what is going on inside and outside of you. Over time, as you review your journal, you may realize patterns and recurring themes that have been hidden from your awareness before. This is when you get a clear picture of what to focus and work on in order to reach higher levels of your growth and evolution.

Community

One of the easiest and most natural ways to slip into a state of joy is to connect and interact with people who resonate with you, inspire you, and give you a sense of self-worth and empowerment. These are your tribal members, the people whom you admire, respect, and care for. They make you come alive and bring out your best self. Finding your tribe and surrounding yourself with true friends is one of the most precious gifts you can receive in life. Take a proactive role to approach people from all walks of life. Be curious in a nonjudgmental way, get to know them, and trust your intuitions. Before you know it, you will start finding and creating your own tribe.

Tension Release Exercise (TRE)

Tension and Trauma Releasing Exercises (TRE) are a series of exercises that assist the body in releasing deep muscular patterns of stress, tension and trauma. The exercises safely activate a natural reflex mechanism of shaking or vibrating that releases muscular tension, which calms down the nervous system and encourages the body to return back to a state of balance. For detailed instructions you can refer to Dr. Berceli's books or go to https://traumaprevention.com/

Laughter Yoga

Laughter yoga, originally developed by Dr. Madan Kataria, is based on the scientific fact that the body cannot differentiate between fake and real laughter. One gets the same physiological and psychological benefits. It is a series of simple exercise routines that is scientifically proven to reduce stress levels by 28% and lower blood pressure by 6%, and generally improves mood and quality of life.

For more information, please refer to Dr. Maden Kataria's book on "Laughter Yoga: Daily laughter practices for health and happiness", or go to https://laughteryoga.org/

PART 2
IMPACT

The underlying character for impact is *strength*. Impact is about creation, making a difference, realizing your powers, taking action, and manifesting your highest vision. Impact is where the rubber hits the road.

What positive impact do you want to make in your life and in other people's lives? Make a list of ideas—short, medium, and long term. It is important to do this exercise before you continue reading the rest of this chapter. Simply giving it a vague round of thinking is not enough. Writing has the inherent effect of crystallizing and clarifying your thoughts. Once you write down your thoughts, you can observe them from a distance, contemplate and ask yourself questions, and review and revise them to clarify and refine your thoughts. Ask questions like, "Is this really what I want? Is there anything else missing? Am I clear and specific enough? Is this really important to me? Why do I want this? Why is this so important to me?" Please take a few minutes to ask yourself these questions before reading further. Bring out your heart's desires without judging or evaluating. You will be reminded again in the practice section of this chapter

"It is the question that drives us." —*The Matrix*

FIRST THINGS FIRST

You start with yourself, and you start now. This is an inside-out process. You cannot hope to make any genuine and lasting positive impact to the world around you unless you have mastered yourself in action. Sometimes people use their actions to project outside of themselves what is lacking inside, in order to convince themselves of their worth and satisfy their ego image, even under the heading of goodwill and service to others. It could be working eighty-hour weeks under the heading of success and commitment, whereas in fact you may be running away from a life of emptiness and isolation. It could be giving away your time and money to charity under the heading of service, whereas in fact you may be searching for self-worth and recognition. It could be addiction to working out, entertainment, video games, or food, whereas these are ways to distract yourself from an underlying lack of meaning and intimacy. These are all compensatory acts of ego, and they do not spring from your true essence, from your abundant self. As long as you are conscious and aware of your underlying motives, and you are honest with yourself, all of this can still help you move closer to the next phase of your evolution. There is no right or wrong, just phases and passages of growth and awareness. Embrace your life as it is now without judgment, while staying curious and inquisitive. Ask yourself questions like, "What areas of my life need more attention? What changes would I want to make to my life? What is the best version of me that is waiting to come out? If a genie appears in front of me, what three wishes would I ask for?"

Write down whatever thoughts and ideas come to you without overanalyzing. It is best to capture whatever comes spontaneously; you can reflect on them later. You can then decide which ones resonate and hold true for you. The intention of this exercise is to give you more clarity on where you are today and where you want to go. It reflects on your current state and desired future state. It is critical to have this clarified as you read on, because without having this solid foundation, it is easy to wander around with no direction or focus, and in spite of exerting much energy and effort, you'll make no real impact.

IDENTIFY YOUR GIFTS

In our self-talk, we are usually experts at pointing out our failures, weaknesses, and shortcomings. But what is much more powerful is identifying and focusing on our strengths and gifts. We all have our own unique gifts, sometimes hidden under a pile of shoulds, obligations, and even shames that were imparted to us throughout our lives. Our society, our communities, and sometimes our families have a peculiar way to mold us into what is accepted as the norm, and they drive away our unique gifts into shadows. All we need to do is look for them, shed light on them, and accept and acknowledge them.

Once you realize and respect your gifts, you start using them and strengthening them more, and gradually you bring out more of the unique you. You carry your gifts with you at all times. You may not be using them consciously, but they are there waiting to be discovered and put to good use. Sometimes you ignore them and label them as unimportant. Sometimes you discard them and label them as impractical. But no matter what you do, they will stay with you in hiding because they are the underlying makeup of the unique you. Reflect on this and review your life from childhood. What qualities, skills, tendencies, and gifts came to you naturally? What came to you as enjoyable, effortless, and easy? What was different about you? What gave you a sense of feeling at home?

I am the youngest of five kids in my family. My parents made a point of hiring a music teacher for each kid based on his or her tendencies. They started my oldest sister with a piano teacher, the next one with a guitar teacher, and so on. It turned out that none of the kids took music seriously and did not have much of an interest to learn an instrument. Every class session was a struggle. By the time it got to me, my parents decided that it was a mute point to force their kids into learning a musical instrument, and maybe it was best to let them be. As a result, I was the only kid in my family who did not have formal music training. However, as I was growing up, there was a piano sitting in our living room, and every once in a while I used to sit and play with the notes. I enjoyed the sounds I was making, the mixture of notes into pleasant tunes and melodies. I loved to play around with the piano. Now, music is a source of joy and inspiration for me, and it plays an important role in my life. I play every instrument I can get my hands on, from various kinds of percussion instruments to piano, guitar, and wind instruments. I don't play at a mastery level, but I enjoy myself, composing music and creating melodies of my soul. I know music is one of my gifts; it came to me naturally. I did not have to force it, and I did not have a music teacher from whom to learn it.

What are some of your gifts? What comes to you naturally? What activities feel effortless and enjoyable to you? Make a list. Again, don't overanalyze; simply write down whatever comes to your mind and review them later. Write them down even if they appear trivial to you. Often we overlook our gifts because it feels so easy and effortless to us, and we think this holds true for everyone else. But often this is far from truth. By undermining our gifts, we are not respecting and recognizing them for what they are.

FULLNESS OF YOUR CREATIVITY

Our souls want to soar. In our hearts, there is a song. In our bellies, there is a power. In our minds, there is a vision. We are meant to live our lives fully and bring out who we really are. We should turn our acorns into magnificent oaks. You might think, "Yeah, right. What about paying the bills that keep piling up every month? What about the unfulfilled relationships that seem to be a recurring theme? What about the realities of life, my boss, my partner, my kids, my health, and my bank account?" Yes, these are all realities of our lives, but I'd like to suggest a different perspective. What if these are all part of the plan? What if they are here to push us into looking beyond and finding our ideal lives? What if they are the cause that forces us into finding our true powers, our gifts, and our missions? What if they are here to help us build character and clarity in order to find our true north?

Victor Frankl, author of *Man's Search for Meaning,* was an Austrian neurologist, psychotherapist, and Holocaust survivor. He lost his whole family and was in Nazi concentration camps for three years under severe conditions.

It can't get much worse than that, can it? Yet he decided to live—and not just live, but live with purpose and personal power. It was during these years that he crystallized his mission in life and developed his theories on logotherapy, which is founded on the belief that human nature is motivated by the search for a life purpose. He decided to make an impact. At the end of the day, it is simply a choice.

"Everything can be taken from a man but one thing: the last of the human freedoms - to choose one's attitude

in any given set of circumstances, to choose one's own way." —*Victor Frankl*

In spite of your circumstances, your challenges, and your limitations, you always have the freedom to make a choice and allow the fullness of your creativity to come into being. Make a choice to rise above your circumstances, even though you don't seem to find the strength to do so. The irony is that once you make the choice to rise up, the power will be there to support you all the way. Remember that when you are engaged in a creative act, you are walking in the unknown territory by design. All your assumptions, expectations, models, and blueprints fall apart. If you are going to bring out your true self, you cannot follow the footsteps of another. You cannot hide in the safe shadows of your parents, gurus, mentors, and role models. Yes, you may feel exposed, vulnerable, and confused at times, but that is exactly how it is if the unique you is allowed to present itself to life.

LIVE THE UNIQUE YOU, COURAGEOUSLY

We are so used to a certain way of conducting our lives that any deviation from it may feel like a resistance and does not feel normal. Over the years, we have established ideas on what is possible and have programmed our minds to stay within the realm of the possible. In circuses, in order to train an elephant, they attach a rope to one of the animal's feet when he is very young. After a while, the baby elephant realizes and accepts that he cannot move beyond what the rope allows. When the elephant grows up, he is still under the control of that same rope even though physically he could easily break the rope if he chooses to. The choice never occurs to him because it is not in the realm of the possibility anymore. When he was young, he tried to break away from the rope many times with no success, and now it is programmed into his brain.

We often behave in a very similar manner. We restrain ourselves with our own self-limiting assumptions and ideas that have formed over time. Our vision of ourselves has become limited: we play small, we play safe, we don't feel deserving of anything more, and we stay in our comfort zone. If we believe in a kind universe, we wait and hope that things will turn around eventually, and that good things will land on our laps. If we believe in a capricious universe, we feel as helpless victims and take no responsibility in owning our experiences. In either case, we strip ourselves of our personal power to make a choice, to consciously respond to the situation at hand with wisdom.

Then there are those courageous moments when we decide to step outside of our comfort zone, but we have the judgment of others to deal with. Even people we love, people we admire, and people we respect may label us as wired, off balanced, risky, bold, and too optimistic. If our connection to our self, to our essence, is weak, then we may easily lose ground, and doubt ourselves and confusion will quickly sneak in. We then quickly snap back into our comfort zone, feeling safe and protected once again. Extending the realm of our possibility is no easy task if we are not grounded in who we are. Fear, uncertainty, and confusion are always going to be there. The question is how we are going to deal with them. Are we going to withdraw and revert back to what we are comfortable with, or are we going to exercise our courage and sense of adventure? Life would be quite boring if everything was predictable. The reality is that there are no guarantees in life, but the more you explore and experiment, the more you access and know your powers, and the more you can live out the unique you and manifest your gifts.

CREATIVE INCUBATION

"There is more to life than increasing its speed."
—*Gandhi*

Our Western culture is geared toward efficiency, productivity, growth, generating results, and doing more in less time. However, there are times in the journey of life when we need to step back, slow down, rest, and reflect. From the outside, nothing is happening and everything is at a standstill, just like a caterpillar hibernating inside the cocoon. This goes against the grain of our culture; it feels very uncomfortable and wasteful to be in this state. We are used to being in control, making things happen, doing, creating, driving, and feeling full of energy and excitement—and this is the opposite end of the spectrum. We feel withdrawn, even depressed and confused. There is no passion, no clarity of purpose. We simply want to be, with not much doing. But this stage is essential in the journey of our transformation. We need to respect it, listen to it, and exercise our patience and compassion to ourselves. If we push ourselves out of this state by force too quickly, we might short-circuit our growth. Because there are no outward signs of positive development, there is an element of trust and respect for the process that needs to be attended to. This is the time to listen to our internal desires and tendencies. Maybe we want to spend more time alone in nature. Maybe we don't want to be around people. Maybe we want to go to a foreign land. Maybe we get an urge to paint, sing, dance. Whatever it is, it is a calling from within that guides us to a path unique to us. We can ignore it and distract ourselves with the usual obligations and duties, or we can respect it and follow it. This is a critical decision because it can either facilitate or thwart our transformation to become new and unique individuals. I call this stage the creative incubation, because a lot is happening inside, at an unconscious level. The creative act is not necessarily being performed by you at a conscious level, but it is being done to you. Therefore there is an element of allowing and not resisting the process. This may not feel comfortable because we like to be in the driver seat; we like to think we are in control. Here, we are asked to stay with the process and allow it to happen, while staying mindful and attentive.

FOLLOW YOUR BLISS

If we allow the creative incubation stage to take its course, it often leads us to our bliss, a term coined by the mythologist Joseph Campbell.

> *"Follow your bliss. If you do follow your bliss, you put yourself on a kind of track that has been there all the while waiting for you, and the life you ought to be living is the one you are living. When you can see that, you begin to meet people who are in the field of your bliss, and they open the doors to you. I say, follow your bliss and don't be afraid, and doors will open where you didn't know they were going to be. If you follow your bliss, doors will open for you that wouldn't have opened for anyone else."* —*Joseph Campbell*

The creative incubation stage has the potential to shed light on your heart's desires, your soul's longing, and your life's purpose. It has been there all along, waiting for you; it is simply a matter of recognizing and following the path. Although following the path is easy and effortless at the heart level, it often opposes with the ego's agendas, and as a result resistance, doubt, and fear take hold. You would need to exercise immense courage and awareness to successfully navigate through the path. By design, it is a path unique to you that has not been travelled before, and therefore it might require walking in the dark forests with no clear sense of where you are heading. Yet there is a deep down knowing that you are on the right path, and there is a process of unfolding that is taking place with every step taken on this path. Although the path seems dark and lonely, there will be seen and unseen helpers and guides appearing in front of you at just the right times. As Joseph Campbell says, doors will open for you. In this phase, the most important character trait to hold is patience and presence, because the process needs to take its own course. The deep-down transformation is not happening in the time and space domain, but at the soul level. It can take weeks, months, or years. Other than allowing and giving ourselves permission to unfold naturally, we don't have much control regarding when and how. Resisting, forcing, or controlling the process has the side effect of blocking or slowing down the flow. The key is to stay mindful every step of the way and integrate the insights that come to us across the multiple dimensions.

Make a Difference

Following your bliss leads to living on purpose. It gives you the clarity and opportunity to play your part on this earth, to live and manifest your life's work. It often involves going beyond the boundaries of your ego self and making a difference on this earth for the benefit of others. It is making a difference by exercising your gifts and acting on your intentions with personal power. This is where you define yourself in action as a conscious creator. It is an inside-out job with the alignment of heart and mind.

Realize that you are making a difference at all times in any case. Every interaction, gesture, and conversation makes a difference. The question is its trajectory and strength of impact. Oftentimes the trajectory and strength of impact is determined by its primary intention and the governing attitude. The story of the brick builder illustrates this well.

A man came upon a construction site where three people were working. He asked the first, "What are you doing?" The worker replied, "I am laying bricks." He asked the second, "What are you doing?" The worker replied, "I am building a wall." As he approached the third, he heard him humming a tune as he worked, and the man asked, "What are you doing?" The worker stood, looked up at the sky, and smiled. "I am building a cathedral!"

Although it may not seem grand at times, don't underestimate the impact you are making to the people around you, to your community, and to your planet. It is an immense responsibility to realize that as a conscious creator, you are making a difference every day by your choices and actions. The power comes when there is alignment between your actions and your words and intentions. This is living in integrity. When there is no conflict within, your energy does not dissipate, and the impact is amplified and laser sharp. It is as if the universe conspires with you to help manifest your intentions. The path opens up, and things happen without much effort. This is when you know you are on your path to bliss and are making an impact every step of the way without even trying. You are making a difference by simply being your authentic self.

LEARN TO SAY NO

We are often surrounded by distractions, demands, and temptations every minute of our lives. If we are not clear and steadfast about our intentions and objectives, it is easy to be the prey. Often we fall into the trap of being nice, and we want to deliver on every request that comes our way. Sometimes we are too optimistic and say yes to anything that comes to us. The combination of being an optimist and being a nice guy can be very damaging. After a while, we may lose ourselves and be unable to find our way back to our own calling, to what is really meaningful and important to us. Say no to people, obligations, requests, and opportunities you're not interested in from now on.

> *"No more yes. It's either 'hell yeah!' or no."* —*Derek Sivers*

It takes a lot of clarity, discipline, and self-worth to say no. By saying yes to only what is meaningful and important to you, you are detoxing yourself from all the noise and focusing your life on what is essential. You start living in alignment with your essence and become more focused and energized. Oftentimes the reason we feel overwhelmed and drained is because we are doing too many things that are not in alignment with our purpose. We are pulled in different directions, and our energy gets scattered and wasted. We may feel helpless and stressed, and we see no way out of this trap, but in fact we have brought this to ourselves by our choices, and we can easily get out of it by making different choices. Reflect on what is consuming you. Simplify your life by saying no to the nonessentials. You will be amazed to realize the amount of energy and clarity you gain once you simplify your life and clarify your priorities.

TAKE ACTION

There are two mental-emotional states that keep you from taking action. The first is doubt. When doubt sneaks in, it dissipates the energy and power of taking action. It opens the door to confusion and takes you away from your position of power. Doubt in itself is a healthy sign. It tells you that there is a misalignment going on, that there is a conflict inside. It tells you that your priorities might not be clear. This is when you need to go back and ask yourself the fundamental questions to gain clarity. However, it is important to make sure you don't turn this into a mental game of procrastination. Sometimes it is important to make the move, even if you are not 100 percent sure. It is okay to make mistakes. That is the only way we can learn and course correct. There is a limit to sitting, thinking, and analyzing.

The second is lethargy. One day you feel excited and committed. You make clear plans and resolve to follow through. But the next day, the energy and conviction is gone. Lethargy has sneaked in, and you have a thousand excuses, most of them logical and valid, to hold off on taking the action to which you were so committed just a few days ago. We have all seen this cycle repeat itself not just during New Year's resolutions but throughout the months and years of our lives. Taking action requires character and the ability to take action long after the excitement of the moment has gone. Character is formed through taking consistent action. Here lies the paradox.

The only way to break this vicious cycle is through the awareness that you can shift your mental state by taking action, even if you don't feel like it. I am sure you have experienced this phenomenon in sports and physical activity. You wake up in the morning and have no desire to get out of bed and do your daily workout. But once you drag yourself up and to the scene, the energy comes with it, and after a while you are charged up. What is important is to be aware that taking action has the ability to change your state of mind. The next time you are lethargic, ask yourself, "How can I exit this state?" Every individual is different, and you need to find your own exit key that works for you. It could be a ten-minute meditation, or listening to five minutes of uplifting music, or watching an inspirational video clip, or taking a nature walk. Maybe you can call up your buddy and get a little inspiration and encouragement. Make a list of activities that help you shift your state of mind to a more empowering and energetic mode. Experiment with it, try new things, see what is most effective for you, and keep practicing. Soon you realize you are no longer at the mercy of your lethargic state of mind, and that you can shift your state at will. The more you do this, the more confident you get, and soon it becomes a part of your character.

PRIORITY AND FOCUS

We all live twenty-four hours days, but have you wondered how some people can be so much more effective, so much more productive, yet so much more grounded and together? One of my challenges in life has been the idea that I want to do everything, I want to live fully, and I don't want to miss out on life's opportunities. I want to spread my wings as far as I can reach. I want to bring out my talents and gifts and sing out my song passionately and impatiently. This all seem very genuine, inspiring, and at times energizing—but in reality I often end up stretching myself too thin and end up empty-handed. I get pulled in all kinds of directions, and I end up feeling frustrated and disappointed about what I actually managed to achieve.

Sometimes doing less is more. Sometimes we need to slow down, in order to go faster. It is all about being clear about our priority and focusing on what is truly important and in alignment with our intentions. It is not about making a long list of to-dos and top-ten priorities. Up until recently, the word *priority* existed exclusively as a singular noun, meaning the very first, or prior. It is only after the 1940s that we pluralize the term and start talking about priorities. Somehow we feel we are now able to have multiple first things. People and companies routinely try to do just that, and they shortchange their success. Our brains are hard wired to concentrate on one thing at a time. Sure, we can do multitasking on trivial or mundane tasks, but it is impossible to concentrate on two tasks at once. The myth of multitasking is that it will make us more effective. In reality, focus and concentration make the difference. We can sequentially focus on multiple tasks by context switching, but that has its costs. If we change focus too often, we are not allowing our bodies and minds to really sink in and get deep into the task at hand. Every time we switch focus, there is an energy dissipation and a start-up time to get into the new focus area. The exception to this is when the tasks are in alignment and synergistic to a primary intention.

If you see the connections and the leverage factor amongst them, it can have a mutual strengthening effect and improve the overall effectiveness. A practical application of this technique is often used by musicians. For example, if an acoustic guitar player also practices on a similar family of instruments, like the mandolin, ukulele, and bass guitar, the speed of learning improves, and the level of creativity increases. If you must have more than one priority, make sure the objectives share a common theme and are in alignment toward your primary intention.

DREAM A NEW WORLD

According to scientists,[5] we have around sixty thousand thoughts a day, and 95–98 percent of them are repetitive and exactly the same as we had the day before. Even more significant, over 80 percent of them are negative. No wonder it is so hard to change a habit or create a new

---

[5] Dr. Joe Dispenza, *You are the Placibo: Making Your Mind Matter* (Hay House, 2015).

lifestyle. This is because most of the time we are not truly conscious; our thoughts and actions are controlled and dictated by our unconscious mind. The moment we pay attention, observe, and become conscious of our thoughts, we have the freedom to make a choice. Only then can we change course and navigate toward a new direction.

The acorn's dream to turn into a giant oak happens naturally and organically as long as the right environment is present; no conscious effort is necessary. But for us, we need to bring our dreams to conscious awareness and turn them into reality by making choices and taking action. It is a creative act. We need to consciously dream a new world and then act on it creatively; otherwise, we keep living the same thoughts, habits, and routines.

The dream is the vision of who you want to be and what you want to bring into this world. It's about bringing out your gifts and living the unique you, creating and bringing forth the best version of yourself. The irony is that you need to believe in yourself and your dream in order to create, and you need to create in order to believe in yourself. It is an interdependent, two-way street, and nothing will change until you start walking on this path. Action is what triggers it. This does not have to be anything grandiose; any small step will do as long as it is deliberate and consistent.

Shamans and sages of the old ages have a practice of reprogramming their unconscious minds with a new dream seed, and by continuously defining and living the dream in their conscious minds, they make a bridge to reality. They hold their visions, unperturbed by outside incidents and circumstances, and they respond to life with their internal attitudes and beliefs. They let life live through them, and so they consciously reshape the reality of their life. Shamans often use rituals to recharge and keep their dreams alive. This could be ceremonies of chanting, dancing, painting, or making a mesa, where they project and imprint their intentions into physical reality.

> *"We are what we think. All that we are arises with our thoughts. With our thoughts we make the world."*
> —Buddha

LIVE YOUR LEGACY

The most important question to ask ourselves is, "Who am I, and why am I here?" We have been conditioned and brainwashed throughout our lives, and so we may have to first reflect on who we are *not*, in order to get closer to the essence of who we really are. It is like peeling an onion, with every layer getting a little closer to the core. Only after we shake off the multitude of our ego-bound images and throw away our artificial masks can we have the courage and insight of knowing who we are. And once we remember, recognize, and know who we are, we can bring it out and live it fully with all our powers, with no hesitations or reservations, and with no compromises.

> *"We must first find the self, the divine, then only can we know what is the work the self or the divine demands from us. As we grow in the inner consciousness, or as the spiritual truth of the divine grows in us, our life and actions must indeed more and more flow from that, be one with that."* —Sri Aurobindo

PRACTICE: CREATE

Through the practice of *creation*, the underlying character of *strength* is turned into its outward manifestation of *impact*. To get any value out of this chapter, it is critical to put the ideas and insights into practice. This is the playground to create the kind of life you want to live. Use these practices to explore what works best for you and integrate them into your life.

> *"The best way to predict the future is to create it."* — *Abraham Lincoln*

Clarity

"What areas of my life need more attention? What changes would I want to make to my life? What is the best version of me that is waiting to come out? If a genie appears in front of me, what three wishes would I ask for?" Write down whatever thoughts and ideas come to you without overanalyzing. It is best to capture whatever comes spontaneously and then reflect on them later. You can then decide which ones really resonate and hold true for you.

_____

_____

_____

_____

_____

Impact

What positive impact do you want to make in your life and in the lives of others? Make a list of ideas—short, medium, and long term. Write down whatever comes to you without overanalyzing or judging. Once you have your list, go back to each of the ideas and ask yourself questions like, "Is this really what I want? Is there anything else missing? Am I clear and specific enough? Is this really important to me? Why do I want this? Why is this so important to me?"

_____

_____

_____

_____

_____

My Gifts

What are some of your gifts? What comes to you naturally? What activities feel to you as effortless and enjoyable? What would you do if you did not have to work for the money? Make a list. Again, don't overanalyze; simply write down whatever comes to your mind and review them later. Write them down even if they appear trivial to you.

_____

_____

_____

_____

_____

Essential

Reflect on what is consuming you. What feels stressful and overwhelming? What activities suck energy out of you? Review your list and cross out the ones that are not essential, the ones that you can live without. Simplify your life by saying no to the nonessential. You will be amazed at the amount of energy and clarity you gain once you simplify your life and focus on your priority.

_____

_____

_____

_____

_____

Legacy

The dream is the vision of who you want to be and what you want to bring out to this world. Bring out your gifts and live the unique you. Create and bring forth the best version of yourself. Live your legacy. Review the vision statement that you came up with in chapter 1's practice section under the heading "Magnet," and make appropriate refinements and adjustments. Make sure it resonates with you.

_____

_____

_____

_____

_____

Action

Review your natural channels of expressions that you came up with in chapter 1's practice section under the heading "Expression." Include other items you feel need to be added. Don't let your rational mind inhibit you with all the reasons it does not make sense. Make a list of what wants to come out. Remember, you don't need to be a painter for you to paint. You don't need to be a dancer for you to dance. You don't need to be a musician for you to play music. Walk on this path with openness and curiosity, and let it carry you to what comes next. Make yourself a plan of action and commit yourself to integrate this into your life.

_____

_____

_____

_____

_____

Fearless

Practice courage once a day. Challenge yourself. Make that call, ask that question, pitch that idea, and post that video. Whatever it is you feel you want to do, do it. The anticipation of the event is far more painful than the event itself. Just do it, and end the inner conflict. Make a list of important things you have been putting off, ignoring, or avoiding. Challenge yourself.

_____

_____

_____

_____

_____

Dare List

Make a list of ideas that stretches your limits. These ideas may seem crazy or unreasonable but can give you a sense of meaning and expansion. Things that deep down, your heart desires but you never felt it is feasible, reasonable, logical or appropriate. You don't dare to do it as you may be afraid what others may think of you. It may seem out of reach, and out of sight. You won't consider it, because you are afraid of failing. This is the time to stretch your imagination and your comfort zone.

_____

_____

_____

_____

_____

Bucket List

Make your bucket list. Things you really want to do before you leave this earth. Places to visit, creative expressions, things to leave behind, connections to make, unfinished business. The experiences you don't want to miss out. Things you want to bring out to this world. How do you want to be remembered?

Most people have it backward: they design their ambitions around their lives, rather than designing their lives around their ambitions. What are the things you absolutely must do before you die? Start there. Then design your life around those things. Or as Covey explained in the *7 Habits of Highly Effective People,* "Begin with the end clearly in mind."

_____

_____

_____

_____

_____

Vision Board

Vision board is a powerful tool to clarify and visualize your ideal future. You can use this exercise to integrate and orchestrate all of your insights and desires in this chapter into a one pager. Use colors, words, shapes, images, pictures, etc. create a vision board that is unique and meaningful to you. Once you completed your creation and are satisfied with it, place it in a spot that you see every day. This will be a great reminder and energizer to stay on target.

_____

_____

_____

_____

_____

Tools and Resources

Drawing

The book *Expressive Drawing: A Practical Guide to Freeing the Artist Within* by Steven Aimone is a good starting point for exploring your drawing and painting talents. You don't need to be a painter to paint, so be open to create your works of art.

Dance

To explore your free expressions of body movement with music, you can participate in a 5Rhythms event near you. There is no need to know how to dance, because it is all about bringing out your free expression through any kind of body movement that feels right to you. This is a dynamic movement practice that ignites creativity, connection, and community (www.5rhythms.com). There are also other variations and offshoots of this practice, including Open Floor (http://openfloor.org) and Ecstatic Dance (http://ecstaticdance.org).

Music

If you have not explored playing a musical instrument before, drumming can provide an easy pathway to creating an energizing and healing experience, especially when it is done in a tribal or group setting. Participating in a drum circle, or creating your own, may be easier than you think. To explore the transformational power of drum beat and rhythmic trance, look into joining a local drum circle or Meetup event near you, or form a drum circle yourself.

Discovering Your Type

There are several personal profile tests that can shed light on our natural tendencies, gifts, and strengths. Myers Briggs (http://www.myersbriggs.org) is one of the most original personality tests based on the works of the psychologist C. G. Jung and his theory of types.

There are other powerful tools, like the Enneagram RHETI test, which can provide valuable insights into our path to self-knowledge (https://www.enneagraminstitute.com). Also, the Disc profile test can help improve our work productivity, teamwork, and communication (https://discprofile.com).

Human Design

Human Design system is based on birth information (exact time and place), and reveals the individual's "design for life", a visual map that illuminates the innate nature, qualities and characters of the person. It uses ancient wisdom (Astrology, I-Ching, Kabbalah, Chakra) and fuses them with modern science (Neutrino physics and genetic coding) to provide a comprehensive and multi-layered take on who we are as individuals. For more information go to https://humandesignforusall.com/

Vision Quest

A modern enactment of an ancient ceremony from native American cultures, rite of passage Vision Quest enables men and women to engage in a sacred journey that can help them find purpose and clarity at critical life transition stages. This could include coming into adulthood, career path transitions, preparing for marriage / having children, or entering elderhood. The Vision Quest program has five core elements that serves as both challenges and supports for the journey: Solitude, immersion in nature, fasting, pan-cultural teachings, and community. For more information go to https://www.ritesofpassagevisionquest.org/

PART 3
ABUNDANCE

The underlying character for abundance is *love*. Abundance is experiencing who you really are at the core. Abundance is participating in the dance of giving and receiving, of sharing. It's living who you are without any hesitations, expectations, or rewards, like a flower that gives out its richness of beauty and fragrance freely and unconditionally. Abundance is letting life live through you with full awareness and no resistance. It is living in accordance to your nature, accessing the powers within, and living a life of strength, prosperity, and inspiration.

TIME AND MONEY

When we talk abundance, the first thing that comes to our minds is money, followed by time. Money and time are currencies that, if applied positively, can lead us to abundance, but by themselves they do not guarantee abundance. We need a balance of both for it to contribute to abundance. One without the other does not help much in creating abundance. I know many people with fat bank accounts who are in a feverish rush to make even more money, but they have no time to nurture their souls. Their narrow definition of success, and the heroic desire to win in this game of fame and fortune, consumes their lives. They can purchase many homes, cars, and toys, but they cannot purchase abundance.

At the other end of the spectrum, we have people with lots of time on their hands who can hardly make ends meet. They may have the philosophy that money is evil and brings corruption. Or they may wish for more money but are not willing to take responsibility of their lives and build the right relationship with money. All the time on their hand turns into waste, and they too have no opportunity to create abundance in their lives.

To live in abundance, it is critical to understand the value of time and money, and to build a balanced and healthy relationship to both. Money is energy, power, and a currency. By itself, it is a neutral energy; you give it meaning by what you decide to do with it. Just like any other source energy, it can be a destructive force that has the capacity to enslave you, or it can be a constructive force that has the ability to free you. Just like any other source energy, you need to understand its governing natural laws in order to harness it. One of the key characteristics of money is fluidity. It naturally wants to flow to fill the gaps and needs, and to create balance. It is generative and comes from an unlimited and unbounded source.

You may take a quick look at our world of money today and say, "This does not jive with the multitude of poverties and tragedies that are going on every day." But our world is the way it is because we made it so. We took this unbounded, fluid energy and made it scarce and concentrated in the hands of the few. We literally blocked the flow of energy from reaching the gaps and needs. We also artificially created a whole bunch of fake and unnecessary needs to redirect the money. We misused this neutral energy and turned it into a powerful monster that controls our lives.

Time gives us an opportunity to be and do. In it resides infinite potential and possibilities. It gives us the freedom to choose, the space to act and create, and the opportunity to make a difference. It is both finite and eternal. As we mentioned in previous chapters, in order to use time effectively, one needs to approach it from two perspectives at the same time. On one side, it needs to be dealt with a sense of urgency to seize the opportunity at hand because time is finite, and once gone, it will never come back. This gives rise to the doing aspect. On the other side of the spectrum, it needs to be dealt with patience and quiet, because time is eternal and can only be accessed at its core through stillness. This gives rise to the being aspect. Life can only be experienced fully when there is an interplay of doing and being at the same time.

Time and money together give us the strength and opportunity to create abundance in our lives and in the lives of others.

CREATE SPACE

Do you have space for abundance? Abundance requires openness and simplicity. Abundance requires transparency and self-respect. You cannot dance your dance when there is no room. A cluttered room full of items does not represent abundance, and a cluttered life full of things does not invite abundance. Abundance is not just collection of things. It is about conducting a life of meaning, harmony, and love.

Observe your life and your home. Does it reflect abundance? Do you have space for it? Are you inviting it in? Your home is a reflection of your life. You can learn a lot about yourself, your motives, and your values by observing and examining your home, the space in which you live. What does your home represent to you? Is it a sanctuary, a refuge, a castle, a place to sleep, a place to show off, a place to hide? What is most important to you in your home? Is it the TV set, your sound system, the view of trees and flowers out the windows, your bedroom, the kitchen? Did you take part in decorating your home—furniture selection, artwork, paintings on the wall—or did you let someone else do it for you? Ask yourself these questions, and more. Inquire and learn more about who you are, what is important to you, and what your home represent to you.

Once you have a good picture, ask yourself, "How can I make space for abundance? How can I use my home to invite more abundance in? What changes can I make to my home in order to facilitate a state of abundance in me?" There is a whole field of feng shui that is based on the Taoist Chinese philosophy of harmonizing people with the surrounding environment and optimizing the energy flow, or chi, in your work or home space. One of the common themes of feng shui in creating more abundance is letting go of extra clutter and detoxing your home. Abundance is like water: it flows where there is space and where there in an invitation of gravity. It follows a natural law; you don't need to force it. You simply need to provide an opening and allow it to flow. It's the same with abundance and money energy. You need to provide a space and open a channel so it can flow. And how do you do that in real life?

BE IN GRATITUDE

One of the key attractors of abundance is gratitude. Being in gratitude is like inviting more of what you are grateful for into your life. What gratitude does for abundance is like what gravity does to water: it allows, it attracts, and it invites that which we are appreciating. It changes our state of mind to be more receptive, to open space for more of it to come in. Gratitude trains your mind to look for what is positive, and it tunes your energy vibration to resonate with what you are grateful for. Unfortunately for most of us, we get to appreciate the value of what we have only when we start losing it. It seems life has its way of teaching us through contrast and duality. We don't quite feel the light unless we experience the dark. We don't quite feel the pleasure unless we experience the pain. It is a matter of how quickly we learn and turn our experiences into wisdom. Being in gratitude cannot be faked; it is not an intellectual exercise. It has to be felt in our bones, and it has to glow out of our hearts. Being grateful leads to happiness, not the other way around. Gratitude is a state of being. There are several ways that can help us reach and maintain a state of gratitude.

The first is remembrance, reminding ourselves of the things we are grateful for on a daily basis. Research has shown that by writing down three things that we are grateful for every day for three weeks, it will significantly impact the level of our happiness[6].

Second, we can broaden our perspective and enlarge our field of vision. Often we feel the grass is greener on the other side. We victimize ourselves and want to get away from where we are and who we are. The Taoist story of an old farmer illustrates this well. One day his horse ran away. Upon hearing the news, his neighbors came to visit. "Such bad luck," they said sympathetically. "Maybe," the farmer replied.

The next morning, the horse returned, bringing with it three other wild horses. "How wonderful," the neighbors exclaimed. "Maybe," replied the old man.

The following day, his son tried to ride one of the untamed horses, was thrown, and broke his leg. The neighbors again came to offer their sympathy on his misfortune. "Maybe," answered the farmer.

The day after, military officials came to the village to draft young men into the army. Upon seeing that the son's leg was broken, they passed him by. The neighbors congratulated the farmer on how well things had turned out. "Maybe," said the farmer.

The wise man's "maybe" signifies a refusal to judge anything that happens. Instead of judging what is, he maintains a higher perspective and a state of equanimity.

The Third way is to find the best in every situation. This is not about fooling or deceiving ourselves about the current situation, but

---

[6] Joel Wong, Joshua Brown, *How Gratitude Changes You and Your Brain* (Greater Good Magazine).

looking for a bright aspect, an opening to light. There is always a trace of an opening in every situation. The key is to look for it and exercise it. Over time, the mind becomes accustomed to finding good in every situation.

LOVE YOURSELF

The state of abundance starts from within. If we are harsh and judgmental about ourselves, we are not promoting a state of abundance, and we are not allowing our goodness to take root and bear fruits. We are often much better at loving others than loving ourselves. When we love someone, we are mindful, respectful, caring, understanding, and encouraging. We focus on their goodness and ignore their darkness. We go out of our way to make them happy without any expectations, and as a result we feel happy. These are all the qualities and behaviors that we need to apply to ourselves.

We find it easier to love someone else partly because we often create an image of the other in our minds that is a projected fantasy. We selectively choose what we want to see and believe. But often our belief in others ignites the goodness in them. It allows them to believe in themselves, and it gives them the permission and courage to expose and experience their best selves. If we can learn to love ourselves in the same way, we have the opportunity to create a growing and nurturing relationship with ourselves. By doing that, we call forth our true selves and allow our authentic selves to come out and shine.

One of the best indications to see whether we are in a loving relationship with ourselves is to observe and pay attention to our self-talk, especially during trying times. For many of us, our voice of judgment is harsh, rigid, and brutal. When something goes wrong, do we blame ourselves, put ourselves down, swear at ourselves, lose our worth, and get angry and frustrated? Or do we treat ourselves with understanding, patience, and respect? We humans have the unique ability to think about what we think about. By observing, examining, and challenging what we think about, we can consciously choose the thoughts that serve us, and reject those that do not. This, like any other skill, needs development and practice, and it is perhaps the single most important skill that contributes to our growth and self-realization.

If we truly examine and challenge our negative thoughts and judgments, we realize that most of these thoughts are based on irrational thinking projected by our fears, wounds, and setbacks of the past. We are letting our past dictate our future and unconsciously keep replaying the scenes of failure and feeling small. however there is no such thing as failure, only learning and growing. The mindset of playing to win is totally different from playing not to lose. One is driven by desire and the other by fear. One is expansive and exploring, and the other is contracting and avoiding. By observing and examining our thoughts, we can consciously shift our perspective and navigate ourselves to a more loving and empowering state, opening ourselves to receiving more abundance.

RESONATE AND ATTRACT

The dream of the acorn is fixed and built-in. We, on the other hand, get to dream our dreams. Our affinities and gifts are planted in us, but how we bring them out to the world and what to make of them is up to us. Planted in us is also the ability to attract our deepest desires in collaboration with the universe. We do this through the principle of resonance and attraction. This principle is at work all the time, whether or not we are aware of it. We have all heard about the law of attraction.

> *"All people, circumstances, events, and situations are attracted to you by the power of the thoughts that you are thinking. Once you understand that you are literally thinking or vibrating things into being, you may discover a new resolve within you to more deliberately direct your own thoughts." —Jerry and Esther Hicks*

Unfortunately, a lot of people misunderstand this principle, and as a result their efforts may lead to frustration and disappointment. The key requirement is vibrational resonance. If you take a string instrument like piano, and play a note, its vibration also excites other strings that resonate with that specific vibration. Although strings are physically separate, the quality of vibrational resonance permeates and excites higher and lower harmonics of the original note.

There is a subtle energy quality communication through resonance that is based on the law of similars, which operates both in the physical and mental world. Many experiments have been conducted to demonstrate the synchronization of brain waves between people working on similar projects, or even thinking of each other.[7] There is an exchange of information with everything within our perception and imagination. When we intend or imagine, we are bringing the object of our intention or imagination into our awareness, and accordingly we enter into resonance with it.

---

[7]   Dean Radin, *Entangled Minds: Extrasensory Experiences in a Quantum Reality* (Paraview Pocket Books, 2006).

Jung coined the word *synchronicity* to describe an acausal connecting principle. This is a major paradigm shift in our current physical reality framework of cause and effect. Here, the effect does not appear because of a sequential series of causes, but rather through a quality of simultaneous resonance, or meaningful coincidences.

The question here is how we create this vibrational resonance that is so critical in manifesting an intention. The most important factors are clarity and purity, intensity and alignment, and response-ability.

CLARITY AND PURITY

We have a tendency to bring to our awareness what we do not want. This does not help with the process—it actually pushes away the desired intention. When we focus on what we do not want, we are in a vibrational resonance to that which we do not want, and therefore we attract more of that into our lives. The key is to catch ourselves and consciously shift our thoughts from what we do not want to what we do want. This step is probably the most important because it is the seed formation upon which the rest of the process builds upon. It is often much easier for us to point out things that we do not like—things that are wrong, unfair, ugly, or stressful. Instead, we need to be able to see and experience the desired state with clarity and ease, and to feel at home with it. This may require some reflective work and soul searching, and that is where purity and authenticity come into play.

There is so much noise out there that we may find it hard to hear our own song, our own sincere desires. A lot of our goals and aspirations are handed down to us and are in reaction to unwanted events or situations. We need to understand our why. Why is it important to us? What does it mean to us? Our intention needs to be genuine and pure. Purity is the quality of its substance, it's realness, its authenticity. It needs to come from within. When our intention is seated and aligned with our hearts' desire, it will have the power to manifest.

INTENSITY AND ALIGNMENT

The other aspect of making an effective vibrational resonance is the intensity and consistency of the intention. By intensity, I do not mean a strong emotional charge of clinging or craving. Rather, it's the strength of focus and concentration, along with persistence and alignment. You may have a clear and pure intention, but if you lack focus and consistency, it can easily be dissipated and lost in the mix.

Often our minds are the battleground for many opposing and conflicting intentions that cancel each other out, and as a result, our primary intention does not get a chance to gain strength in order to produce resonance. When intention is not rooted at the heart level, doubt can easily enter the picture and scatter the focus and concentration. Like any other skill, the ability to stay focused and steadfast can be acquired and strengthened through ongoing practice.

Meditation, through all its forms, is a great tool to help with concentration and focus. The mind of a beginning meditator is crowded and full of chatter. Most meditation techniques start by focusing the mind on one thing. It could be a flame, a mantra, or in the case of mindfulness meditation, observing our breath going in and out. Initially it seems impossible to focus even for a minute. The mind acts like a crazy monkey, jumping all over the place. That is where I was when I started on a ten-day Vipassana silent meditation retreat many years ago. There was nothing else on the agenda but meditation. Initially it was a struggle to sit and meditate for twelve to fourteen hours per day. But with patience and practice, I realized that the mind can be trained gradually, hour by hour, day by day. Toward the end of the ten-day retreat, my focus was laser sharp, and I was able to focus my mind without perturbations for the full hour. That was something that I could not imagine was possible at the beginning of the retreat.

RESPONSE-ABILITY

Response-ability acts as a bridge between the world of mind and matter. You may have a clear and pure intention. You may even have a focused and consistent intention. But if you don't respond to the signs and act on the offerings and callings that come to you, you cannot close the loop and bring your intention to reality. The ability to respond requires us to be mindful of what is happening inside and outside ourselves, see the connections, seize opportunities, make choices, and follow with action. One cannot sit in the cave and expect things to be different. We are co-creators of our reality and need to take active roles during the process of manifestation. It is a participatory act at both conscious and unconscious levels.

Responding does not always mean taking an action or doing something. It may simply mean being mindful of the present moment's reality, being in tune with what is happening, noticing the signs, listening to guidance, receiving insights, integrating them into our lives, and preparing ourselves for what is to come.

PATIENCE

There is a fine line between participating and controlling. Often we are so focused on the results that we start pushing, pulling, and using brute force. Once we have clarity and purity in our intention and create focus and alignment, we need to let go of attachments to specific outcomes. We need to hold a flexible and trusting mindset and know that everything has its time to flourish. We cannot expect an apricot tree to bloom and bear fruit without going through its seasons of growth and maturation. Patience calls for wisdom, and it invites us to see the whole picture, to take the time and notice, care, and sit with a situation patiently until it's wisdom is revealed. Patience helps us stay anchored and grounded, as we allow the universe to take its course. Patience is a required ingredient in the participatory act of co-creation. It calls for a conscious and proactive stance to be in the state of readiness without the tension or expectation. It calls for letting go of attachment to results while holding space for the original intention.

BALANCE

Being in balance is not a static state; it requires constant awareness and mindfulness. Just like the rope walker who is fully present and responds to minute shifts of body weight on the rope to find its balance, we need to stay awake and fluid to our lives to find our balance. And balance is a very personal thing. What is balance for one, may be off balance to another. We need to be open to experimentation across multiple polarities to find our own balance.

An abundant life is where all aspects of our lives are in synergy and in balance. This is a dynamic state where each aspect of life is in harmony with the other and creates a whole that is much more powerful and beautiful than the sum of its parts. Like a skilled painter bringing together the balance of shapes and colors to create a beautiful painting, we create our lives of balance with a synergistic brushstroke of our thoughts, words, and actions.

GIVE AND RECEIVE

The path of self-realization starts from yourself, but eventually it leads to an act of self-transcendence, an act of service. Through connecting to your self, you realize that we are all connected at the core. Through honoring yourself, you learn to have respect and reverence for all. You go beyond yourself and reach out to the other. That is where the joyous celebration of giving and receiving starts.

> *"Each of us are angels with only one wing. We can only fly embracing each other."* —Luciano Decrescenzo

The act of giving and receiving turns into a circle of no beginning and no end. Giving becomes receiving, and receiving becomes giving. This is the most outwardly visible aspect of living in abundance. When you live in abundance, you want to participate and engage in the feast of giving and receiving at all times. Where to give becomes a gifting of the heart, with no expectations or strings attached, like the flower giving away its fragrance freely and naturally. Receiving carries no burden or obligations with it, no promises or return favors with it. It's like the meadows receiving the rain from the sky with an open heart, with gratitude, appreciation and joy.

> *"I slept and dreamt that life was joy. I awoke and saw that life was service. I acted and behold, service was joy."* —Tagore

HONOR YOURSELF

One of the main blockages on our path to abundance is that we feel we don't deserve it and are not worthy of it. We'd rather stay small, stay invisible. We are not seeing and honoring our greatness.

> *"It is our light not our darkness that most frightens us. We ask ourselves, who am I to be brilliant, gorgeous, talented and fabulous? Actually, who are you not to be? You are a child of God. Your playing small does not serve the world. There is nothing enlightened about shrinking so that other people won't feel insecure around you. We were born to make manifest the glory of God that is within us."* —Marianne Williamson

We need to learn to embrace ourselves fully—our lights and our shadows, our strengths and our weaknesses, our joys and our sorrows. We must realize there is nothing to hide, nothing to be ashamed of. Let's honor ourselves fully and completely, just the way we are. Let's appreciate our own uniqueness and respect our differences. There is no need to be someone else but yourself, no reason to wait for some other time but now, and no desire to be someplace else but here.

Honoring ourselves is practicing acceptance, respect, and compassion toward ourselves. It's going beyond the surface and reaching and honoring our cores with mindfulness and reverence. It's realizing that everything happens for a reason, and we can use every situation for discovering and bringing out our powers.

PRACTICE: CELEBRATE

Treat the practices in this section as ways to engage and celebrate life, to participate in the game of giving and receiving, as a way to allow more abundance to flow into your life. Through practice of celebration, the underlying character of love manifests itself as abundance.

Success

What does success mean to you?

What is your relationship with money in this context?

Is it working for you? And if not, what would you shift in your perspective to enhance your relationship with money so that it can better serve you?

_____

_____

_____

_____

_____

Random Acts of Kindness

Get into a habit of doing random acts of kindness throughout your days and weeks. This does not need to be anything grandiose. It could be small gestures or words of encouragement. It could be reaching out to another and offering support, or extending our arms to give a simple hug. The key is to do the act with absolutely no expectations or need for recognition. You will be surprised how these simple acts of kindness can transform your psyche and open you to more abundance.

_____

_____

_____

_____

_____

Share Your Gifts

How can you participate in the game of giving and receiving? What gifts of yours are you willing to offer and share with the world? This does not have to be a thing; it could be as simple as being there for someone to listen to and providing support. It could be showing compassion and inspiration to someone in struggle. What are some ways you can share your gifts?

_____

_____

_____

_____

_____

Love

How can you shift your perspective to seek to love more than to be loved? Byron Katie says, "If I had a prayer, it would be this: God spare me from the desire for love, approval, and appreciation. Amen."

The irony is that as soon as we genuinely shift our perspective, we will experience the world as more loving and supportive to us.

_____

_____

_____

_____

_____

Honor Yourself

What are some of the characteristics that you don't appreciate in yourself? Often our dark shadows are there for a good reason. By accepting, understanding, and integrating our shadows into our psyche, we become more whole and powerful. How can you embrace and honor yourself more, the whole of you, without judgment and with full acceptance? How can you allow yourself to be more expansive and grand?

_____

_____

_____

_____

_____

Gratitude

Write three things that you are grateful for each day for the next three weeks. Call this a gratitude journal. Be consistent and keep at it. Research has shown that this simple act makes us happier and healthier over time. By conducting this simple daily practice, you are establishing a habit of being grateful, which leads to a state of grateful living.

_____

_____

_____

_____

_____

Abundance

How can you open space for more abundance to flow into your life? Do an audit of your beliefs, your home, and your work. Remember that once you create an opening, abundance flows in naturally. Ask yourself what is currently blocking the flow of abundance to come in. Evaluate your beliefs, habits, and lifestyle. Look for self-imposed limitations and restrictions. How can you shift your perspective away from scarcity and invite more abundance into your life?

_____

_____

_____

_____

_____

TOOLS AND RESOURCES

Feng Shui

Feng shui is the study of the relationship between the environment and human life. It enables you to influence interacting energies to achieve balance and harmony in order to achieve specific life improvements. The book *Feng Shui for Dummies* offers a good introduction to the concept and how you can apply theses principle in your life.

The Work

Byron Katie's "The Work" is a simple yet powerful process of inquiry that teaches us to identify and question the thoughts that cause us our suffering in the world. For further info or to sign up for an event near you, go to http://thework.com.

Psychosynthesis

Psychosynthesis, developed by the psychiatrist Roberto Assigioli, is drawn from many traditions of the East and the West. It is a process for personal growth, with the principle goal of integrating and harmonizing all aspect of ourselves into a single whole. Check out https://www.psychosynthesis.org for more information.

Gratitude App

There are a multitude of mobile apps that can help you get into the habit of recording what you are grateful for on a daily basis. Some examples are "Grateful: A Gratitude Journal and Private Diary" and "Gratitude Journal 365."

Brain Sync

Brain sync technology is a simple way to drive brain activity into high level states of mind (alpha, beta, theta, and gamma) in order to tap into your inherent potential and unleash your power to think, create, heal, and change (http://www.brainsync.com).

The Three Principles

The three principles of Mind, Consciousness and Thought was first introduced by Sydney Banks in an attempt to bring a shift in our understanding of the nature of human existence and of human psychological functioning. Since then, the Three Principles Movement across the globe, along with the Three Principles Foundation, a not- for-profit organization, are dedicated to help relieve human suffering and raise mankind's awareness through the understanding of the Three Principles. For more information go to http://threeprinciplesfoundation.org/

PART 4
FREEDOM

97

PART 4
FREEDOM

97

The underlying character for freedom is health. Health and healing are both derived from the Anglo-Saxon root word *hal*, meaning "whole" and "holy". Being healthy is being in the state of wholeness, free from restrictions and limitations across physical, mental, emotional, and spiritual levels. Free from the past or the future, and living in the now.

PRISONERS OF OUR MINDS

Our recent scientific revolution and technological advancement has led us to a reductionist mindset and specialization approach. Our doctors are trained and specialized in one narrow aspect of the body, and often only a specific aspect of a body part or function. Within each specialization, they go into sub-specialization categories that take them to even deeper and narrower levels. Although amazing information and knowledge has been gathered through this approach, we have lost the understanding of the big picture, the wholeness of our being. Through this reductionist and mechanical mindset, we have made ourselves blind to the interdependencies, interactions, and mysterious workings of the whole.

Many of our modern diseases, sufferings, and tragedies are the direct result of the fact that we have lost touch with the whole. We are exploiting and mistreating the earth, not knowing that we are slowly digging our own graves in the process. We are medicating ourselves with various drugs to suppress our symptoms, not realizing that we are creating worse side effects and damaging the body's own healing mechanism. Our reductionist and narrow focus has turned us into self-centered beings, seeking short-term gains and living in isolation from ourselves, others and the earth.

The problem is that in this process, we became so sure of ourselves and our knowledge base that we no longer question ourselves. If we don't understand a phenomenon with our current level of reasoning and scientific understanding, we easily discard it and name it voodoo or superstition. By doing so, we close the door to the world of mystery and awe, and the wisdom of the whole. In a sense, we have become prisoners of our minds and our belief systems. We only see and experience the aspects of the reality that fit with our current belief system, and we are blind to the rest.

LOOK AT THE WHOLE

The whole can be very different from the sum of its parts. Take the magnificent painting of Michelangelo on the Sistine Chapel ceiling, which upon reflection, invokes joy and beauty in us. We can't quite explain what it is, but we know it is something beyond the mechanical placement of colors and shapes next to each other. It is as if the painting carries a soul, a divinity, a presence of its own. Its existence reaches beyond the borders of a wall or canvas, and it touches our hearts and souls, triggering our hidden memories, dreams, longings. It opens doors to other realms that we did not know existed.

We can only perceive the whole when we are present as a whole, engaging all of our channels of perception and awareness. If we use only our rational minds, we will perceive only that aspect of the reality and miss out on the whole. The whole reveals itself to us when we fully reveal ourselves to it, opening our minds, hearts, intuition, feelings, and senses in harmony to each other. That is when we can get a glimpse of the interactions and interconnectedness of each of the individual pieces that contribute to the makings of the whole.

Our bodies are undoubtedly the most complex system in the world, and have been the subject of study and exploration throughout history in an attempt to restore and maintain the state of optimum health. Ancient Egyptians developed their theory of channels that carried air, water, and blood to the body; they believed if the channels were blocked, it would create signs of disease and feeling unwell. In traditional Chinese medicine, the energy meridian system, also known as channel network, are paths through which the life energy, known as qi or chi, flows. The study of acupuncture, acupressure, qigong, and tai chi are based on this principle and belief that restrictions and blockages to the flow of energy through our meridian system are the cause of physical and psychological diseases. In traditional Indian philosophy, chakras, or energy points, are the meeting points of the subtle energy channels called Nadi, which are believed to be channels in the subtle body through which the life force, or vital energy, moves.

In Ayurvedic medicine, the balance between elemental substances, called Dosas, are of key importance. Any imbalance or suppression of natural urges is considered unhealthy and can lead to illness. In the field of homeopathy, symptoms are considered signs of an imbalance, and the role of the healer is to study the totality of the symptoms in order to understand the underlying cause for the imbalance, rather than suppressing the symptoms. The underlying principle in all of these disciplines is to work with the body to remove blockages and imbalances, and as a result, reactivating the body's own healing mechanism.

MAGIC OF HEALING

When we injure ourselves or get a cut on our skin, we usually clean the area and put a bandage on it. But have you ever wondered what happens underneath the bandage? If you take moving pictures over time and then watch the movie, it looks more like watching Wolverine heal his body in the X-Men movies. It is magic. The only thing we did was keep the area clean and away from outside invaders, so that the body can do its work. The power of our self-healing mechanism is at work all the time. Recovery from a surgery, broken bone, infection, and flu are examples of the body's healing mechanism at work. The most effective role a practitioner can play is to create an environment that is conducive to healing, and to stimulate the body's own healing mechanism to heal itself.

In modern cybernetics, there is a fundamental principle that states any highly organized system reacts to stress always by producing the best possible response that it is capable of in the moment. If you apply this principle in the human being, this means that the defense mechanism makes the best possible response to the disease-causing stimuli, which is often manifested as symptoms. For any therapy to be effective, it would make sense for that the practitioner to cooperate with this process and help facilitate the process by providing the right environment and resources.

However, the approach in Western medicine is often the opposite. The minute we see a symptom, we rush to suppress and mask the symptom by drugs and medications. We don't even give ourselves a chance to understand the root cause of the imbalance in the first place. In a sense, this is an insult to our body's intelligence. If you see the oil engine light on the dashboard of your car turn on, you take it to the mechanic to fix it. How would you feel if the mechanic simply cut the wires to the light so that it turned off? Would you thank him and drive away? This is exactly what happens in most of our doctor visits today.

MY JOURNEY OF SELF HEALING

I had a severe back injury over twenty years ago. On a fine summer day, I was out in our backyard doing some landscaping. I wanted to move a big rock to a new location and asked my wife for help. She took a quick look at the big rock and said, "No way am I going to touch this rock." Being the impatient and egocentric person that I was, I decided to do it all by myself. I gave it all my strength, and the next thing I remember, I was flat on my back in unbearable pain. My wife drove me to the emergency room. Two of my disks were severely herniated, and upon examination, I was told that due to the severity of the damage, I had to go through a serious surgery to diffuse metal steel rods into my vertebrae, with a slight risk of getting paralyzed. I did not quite like the idea, and over the next few weeks, I kept seeing other medical doctors, back specialists, and neurologists with the hope of finding an alternative to surgery. After examining me and checking my CT scan and MRI results, they all recommended the same surgical procedure. In the meantime, in spite of being on multiple pain drugs, I was not able to stand up for more than a few minutes, and I was in severe pain. Nevertheless, I kept seeking more opinions.

I think it was doctor number seventeen who, after examining me, looked me in the eye and said, "If you can withstand the pain, there is a chance that your body can heal itself." That was the seed of hope I was looking for, and it started me on my journey of self-healing. The first thing I did was sign up for a master certificate program to learn hypnotherapy in order to manage my pain through self-hypnosis. Next, I signed up for a ten-day Vipassana silent meditation retreat. I started my research and training to learn about visualization, Reiki, physical therapy, homeopathy, Ayurveda, and acupuncture. I used myself as a guinea pig to experiment on.

Long story short, within six months I was back playing tennis, and to this day, I am in gratitude for having a healthy back. This experience gave me amazing insights and wisdom into the workings of my own body, as well as its interaction and interdependencies with the world of mind and spirit.

Having said that, I have no intention of berating the value of Western medicine. There are times when approaches of Western medicine are the only viable option to consider, especially in emergency and critical situations. The key is to have a broad perspective and understanding of all available options, and to create an integrative plan that works for the specific situation.

HEALTH IS FREEDOM

Optimum health can be defined as freedom from limitations and restrictions across physical, mental, emotional, and spiritual levels.

At the physical level, it is freedom of movement, building strength, flexibility, durability, agility, and balance. It is creating a refined body that is the conduit for the flow of vital energy.

At the mental level, it is clear thinking, building on all mind powers of memory, reflection, analysis, and creativity. It is being free from judgment and dogma. It's being free from the programming of culture, parents, and peers. It's the ability to think outside of the box and have a calm and quiet, yet alert and attentive mind. Rather than our thoughts controlling us, we must be the master of our thoughts and use this magnificent creative power to manifest our reality in alignment with our hearts' desires.

At the emotional level, it is freedom of expression. It's the ability to express and experience all ranges of feelings and emotions, using them as guides to learn about ourselves and others. It involves removing emotional blockages and feelings of being stuck. Celebrating who we are and the way we are, and having the courage and freedom to bring out the song within and dance with it joyously.

At the spiritual level, it is being connected to our essence and living our purpose. It is being able to observe the reality as it is, without cravings or aversions, and free from attachments. It is creating and serving without ego, being present in the moment, and following our bliss.

These levels are all interrelated and integrated, with each affecting the other—hence the criticality of having a holistic view of the person. Any dis-ease in any of the levels will create an imbalance and limitation in the whole. Any enhancement or improvement in any of the levels will bring about harmony and wellness to the whole.

The underlying operating principles of modern medicine is based on a reductionist approach and is about desperate intervention rather than prevention, symptom suppression rather than root cause analysis. However, in recent years there has been an increased awareness and shift toward a whole-health model. The increasing rates of chronic illnesses and the failing health care system, which is actually more like a sick care system, has led to doubts and questions about the whole approach. Initiatives and efforts on functional medicine, integrative medicine, complementary and alternative medicine, and energy medicine are positive steps toward creating a more holistic view of health and healing. Several hardcore-trained MDs of the West are looking at the hard facts, scratching their heads, researching and exploring other avenues, and bringing their findings back to the masses. Unfortunately, the marketing spending of pharmaceuticals and the staying power of the institutions are so strong and incumbent that it makes the process of transformation difficult and challenging.

It's Simple

Many insightful research studies and excellent books have been written by the new breed of doctors and health practitioners who were able to question the status quo, go outside of their comfort zones, and focus on the evidence. They have brought together a broader understanding of health and what we need to do in order to avoid and reverse chronic illnesses, stay healthy, and thrive in our lives. Dr. Colin Campbell's *China Study* is one of the most comprehensive studies on nutrition conducted. Dr. Mark Hyman's *Functional Medicine* is an attempt to look at the whole and better understand the interactions between the body parts and functions. Dr. Kenneth Pelletier's *New Medicine* brings about alternative therapies to create an integrative approach to health. Dr. Joel Fuhrman, Joshua Rosenthal, Brendan Braizer, Rip Esselstyn, Deepak Chopra, and many others have brought great insights and findings into the picture. At first glance, the information might seem disjointed, complicated, and overwhelming. However, from a practical point of view, there is a common ground and an amazing synergy and alignment in their core messages. It all boils down to a very simple set of guidelines and recommendations.

Although for simplicity and clarity, I am summarizing them under separate headlines of physical activity, nutrition, mental, emotional, rest, and meaning, I'd like to reiterate the overriding principle of wholeness: that they are all connected and interrelated. Also, rather than following a set of predetermined, strict rules and regiments, I'd like to point out the importance of understanding each person's individual needs and constitutional makeup. Our bodies carry an amazing level of intelligence and inherent knowing, and if we only learn to listen and respect our own bodies, we will find our own answers.

PHYSICAL ACTIVITY

In modern society, we are spending too much time sitting in front of a screen, sitting in traffic, or sitting in meetings. US teenagers average about nine hours a day in front of a screen, excluding the time that is spent at school or doing homework. We prefer to pay someone else to do our yard work, vacuum our homes, and even do our shopping so that we can have more time sitting in front of a screen. A sedentary lifestyle has led to severe issues, including obesity, depression, anxiety, and many other chronic diseases.

There is ample research and evidence that shows[8] allocating thirty to sixty minutes a day doing moderate exercise reduces diabetes by 58 percent, anxiety by 48 percent, depression by 47 percent, heart disease by 50 percent, and progression of dementia and Alzheimer in older patients by 50 percent. Other than health benefits, physical activity also helps with stress management, better sleep, and mental clarity, and it gives us more energy and vitality.

For optimum physical performance and agility, it is important to not only increase the duration and intensity of the activity, but to also include a variety of exercises to optimize full body performance. These include aerobics, stretching, strength building, and balance exercises and activities.

Further studies have shown that thirty to sixty minutes of moderate

---

[8]   Dr. Mike Evans, "*23 1/2 Hour:* What Is the Single Best Thing We Can Do for Our Health," https://ed.ted.com/featured/Mot8KdLT.

exercise for a minimum of five days per week gives the biggest return on investment on health. The key is to integrate this into your daily routine and pick activities that give you a fun and enjoyable experience. It could be as simple as walking the dog, hiking, gardening, playing tennis, dancing, or taking the stairs instead of the elevator to work. If you enjoy the outdoors, why not do biking or hiking rather than forcing yourself to go to an indoor gym? If you like nature, why not do some gardening and yard work? If you have small kids, why not make a habit of doing some physical activities with them. Doing your daily exercise does not necessarily require an elaborate setup or sophisticated equipment, or even a specific time of the day. Make it a fun ritual that you look forward to every day.

NUTRITION

The importance of nutrition to our well-being cannot be overstated. After all, we are what we eat. In six to eight months, the body nearly completely regenerates itself at the cellular level. Without the healthy nutritional building blocks, the body lacks the components to regenerate itself effectively. Our poor eating habits of consuming foods with low nutrient density, paired with overconsumption of sugar and processed foods loaded with chemicals, puts a huge amount of nutritional stress on our bodies.

According to the National Institute of Health, over 70 percent of Americans are considered obese or overweight. Every day there is a new weight-loss diet, often with conflicting information and recommendations. The weight-loss industry was a $64 billion market in 2014. There has been a fixation in our society on losing weight rather than staying healthy. A lot of the "lose weight" diets may help you lose weight, but they can actually damage your health. Losing

Path to Freedom

weight does not necessarily mean being healthy. What is important is to focus on your health rather than your weight.

With that in mind, let's explore the kind of diet that promotes health and well-being. There has been scientific proof and abundant evidence that people who eat mostly animal-based foods get more chronic diseases, and people who eat mostly plant-based foods are the healthiest and tend to avoid chronic illnesses. Dr. Campbell sums up the recommendations in one sentence: "Eat a whole foods, plant-based diet, while minimizing the consumption of refined foods, added salt and added fat."[9]

Believe it or not, the most nutrient-rich foods are plants, not animals. Broccoli has twice as much protein as steak. Another problem with meat protein is that it comes with saturated fat and cholesterol. However, plants don't have nearly as much marketing as meat.

Changing your eating habits and making healthy choices doesn't need to be difficult. You don't need to be obsessed with calorie counting, or be hard on yourself by following strict regiments. Eating is meant to be an enjoyable experience. If you are stressed out about eating, your digestive system is compromised. How you eat is as important as what you eat. The table below can help you make the transition from unhealthy foods to healthy, nutrient-rich foods. The idea is to have over 90 percent of your food intake be in the "increase" category of healthy, nutrient-rich foods.

---

[9]   T. Colin Campbell and Thomas M. Campbell, *The China Study* (Ben Bella Books, 2006).

REDUCE
Sugar (avoid processed, refined sugar)   **Refined carbohydrates** (pastas, bread)   **Dairy** (milk, cheese)   **Meat** (prefer wild fish)   **Cakes and pastries**   **Caffeine and alcohol**
INCREASE
Leafy greens (spinach, kale, Lettuce, Arugula)   **Fruits** (orange, apple, avocados, berries, pepper)   **Flowers** (broccoli, cauliflower)   **Roots** (carrots, potatoes, beets, onions)   **Legumes** (beans, peas, lentils, soybeans)   **Mushrooms** (portabella, shiitake, white bottom)   **Nuts and seeds** (walnuts, almonds, cashew, flax, sunflower)   **Whole grains** (wheat, brown rice, corn, oat)

As you work toward developing more healthy eating habits, it is important to consider the following points.

– Modern-age obsessions with efficiency and mass production have lead to food production methods that are not healthy and are in some cases toxic. If we are not careful about where and how our food is produced, we may be consuming a lot of chemicals, hormones, pesticides, antibiotics, and preservatives along with our main dish. It is always best to choose naturally grown, organic foods, especially fresh, locally grown fruits and vegetables.

– The body is 75 percent water, and so it makes sense that this essential fluid must be continually replenished. We can go without food for over a month, but we cannot live without water for more than a couple of days. Make it a habit of drinking six to eight glasses of clean, filtered water every day.

– Many health-conscious people are obsessed with taking loads of various supplements. However, you cannot make unhealthy diets into healthy ones by taking supplements. The human body has an amazing natural ability to create what it needs out of healthy, nutrient-rich food. If you feed yourself with healthy, nutritious building blocks, you will not need to worry about supplements.

– There are people who have sensitivity and negative reactions to certain kinds of foods; these may include gluten, dairy products, and nuts. The best way to find out is to experiment and eliminate such foods from your diet for a few weeks; then reintroduce them individually and observe the effects on your state of health.

MENTAL

"Mind is everything. What you think, you become."
—Buddha

Ever since the era of Cartesian dualism, founded by Descartes and Newton, our worldview has been of the separation of mind and matter. It was accepted that the laws and principles that govern the world of matter are totally separate and different from the world of the mind. It is only through the dawn of quantum physics and the works of Einstein and Heisenberg that this belief system is being challenged. The implications of this paradigm shift are just beginning to manifest itself in our everyday lives. The law of attraction, observer effect, placebo effect, neuroplasticity, epigenetics, energy healing, and spontaneous remissions are among the many examples that point to a new way of looking at the world of mind and matter. It's the view that mind and matter are indeed interconnected and entangled, and that both are made up of the same vibrational source energy.

One of the most important shifts that this mindset offers is realizing the creative powers of the mind and its potential to influence reality. Intention is an act of creation. We literally think ourselves and our reality into being. We choose our experience from the quantum field of infinite possibilities by giving it our intention and attention. This is happening at all times, whether or not we know it. The only difference is that some of us are more conscious of this mechanism at work than others. Once we truly internalize and embrace this worldview, we can slowly step out of our victim stories and limiting beliefs and claim our powers to be the master of our thoughts and our lives.

We often zap our vitality, curiosity, and creative powers by allowing negative thoughts and judgments into our minds. Daniel Amen calls this an ANTs infestation—Automatic Negative Thoughts. The key to moving away from ANTs is to get out of the mindless autopilot mode and into a state of inquiry. Having the ability to observe and catch ourselves having a negative thought or a limiting belief, and then putting them up for investigation. Ask yourself, "Are these thoughts completely true? Are these thoughts serving me?" If they are not, choose to not engage with that thought and consciously shift your thoughts to a more positive and empowering state. Like anything else, this may require some practice. As you practice, you begin to catch your ANTs faster and faster, and after a while you don't even go there in the first place.

One of the most effective tools to help strengthen your mind muscle is mindfulness meditation. The practice of mindfulness is about getting in touch with your own experience moment to moment in a nonjudgmental and unattached way. It is observing your thoughts and experiences as they occur, without attaching any stories or emotional charges to them. You can practice mindfulness anywhere and anytime—while sitting, walking, or eating. At first it may require some discipline to stay focused and consistent, but after a while, it can turn into a daily ritual practice, and it becomes effortless and second nature.

Another important practice is what I call mental workout. Keep your mind open and growing at all times. Stay curious, ask questions, try new things, learn new skills, and challenge yourself and your assumptions. Sometimes it is a lot more liberating and powerful to question your answers rather than answer your questions. Our minds have an amazing capacity to regenerate and upgrade themselves through these practices. Perhaps the only limits to the human mind are those in which we believe. By using the power of our imagination, we can stretch our boundaries, challenge our current limiting beliefs, and create a new reality.

In the field of neuroplasticity, there is a principle that states, "Neurons that fire together, wire together." This phenomenon holds true whether or not the experience is real or imaginary. A recent research study brings this to life.[10] It was demonstrated that the subjects who mentally rehearsed one-handed piano exercises for two hours per day for five days—but never actually touching any piano keys—demonstrated almost the same brain changes as people who physically performed the identical finger movements on a piano

---

[10]   Dr. Joe Dispenza, *Breaking the Habit of Being Yourself* (Hay House, 2013).

keyboard for the same length of time. Functional brain scans showed that all the participants activated and expanded clusters of neurons in the same specific area of the brain. In essence, the group who mentally rehearsed practicing scales and chords grew nearly the same number of brain circuits as the group who physically engaged in the activity. We literally can upgrade, rewire, and reprogram our brains at will. At the highest evolutionary stage, we get to create and choose our experiences, irrespective of external circumstances.

EMOTIONAL

We all carry emotional wounds and traumas as we go through life. Some of them are inflicted upon us through external circumstances, and some are self-inflicted by our own interpretations of the incidents. In either case, we carry these emotional knots within us, and they restrict our freedom to fully experience life. Our instinctive reactions to these wounds are to protect ourselves by keeping them out of our conscious minds, so we don't remind ourselves of the pain and suffering. As a result, these wounds get pushed deep into the subconscious mind, where they run our lives in the background without our notice.

The only way to release ourselves from their grip is to bring them out of their hiding and into the light to realize that they can all be instruments for our own growth and evolution. For every loss, there is a gain. For every sadness, there is a joy. It is simply a matter of time and awareness. If we can go beyond the duality of pain and pleasure, we can free ourselves to experience life fully with its broad spectrum of emotions. Knowing that we all experience these emotions at one time or another allows us to drop our masks, open our hearts to each other, and realize that we are all connected at the core. This sense of connection is something that most of us have lost in modern society. We work in our cubicles, communicate through our computer screens, and connect to the world through our TV screens. We are missing out on the intimacy, on the physical and emotional connection that is so critical for our well-being. There is mounting research evidence linking loneliness to physical illness, depression, and functional and cognitive decline, and it's a predictor of early death. Lisa Rankin calls loneliness the number one public health issue of our time.[11]

Loneliness does not necessarily mean being physically alone. Many of us conduct lonely lives in the midst of being with others. We tend to maintain superficial conversations and interactions in order to stay away from being vulnerable, and as a result we rob ourselves of having intimacy and creating a deeper connection with another person. We all need a sense of belonging and a sense of community. If we hold a space of nonjudgment and acceptance for others while remaining in our own truth and authenticity, we will have the opportunity to heal each other.

REJUVENATION

In the modern age, we are constantly bombarded with loads of information, stimulations, and demands on a daily basis. We seem to always be in the catch-up mode. We're expected to do more, run faster, and be more efficient and productive. However, the non-doing is as important as the doing part. We need to allow ourselves time to rest, reflect, and rejuvenate. Sometimes we need to slow down in order to go stronger.

---

[11] Lissa Rankin, *Mind Over Medicine: Scientific proof that you can heal yourself* (Hay House Inc., 2014).

A lot of us take for granted the importance of a good night's sleep to our well-being. With all the pressures and responsibilities of our lives, often the first thing that gets compromised is the quality and quantity of our sleep. Although it may not seem like it, a lot happens while we sleep. During sleep, the body repairs and restores itself, the brain releases hormones that encourage tissue growth, and the body makes more blood cells, which enhances the immune system. After a good night's sleep we are rejuvenated, our minds are more clear and sharp, our emotional state is more positive and energized, and we feel more grounded and empowered to tackle the challenges of the day. The results of a 2016 study released by the Centers for Disease Control and Prevention indicated more than one-third of American adults are not getting enough sleep on a regular basis. Although the general recommendation for adults is to get seven to nine hours of sleep each night, the optimum hours of sleep for each person may vary based on age and constitution. Also, the quality of sleep is as important as the quantity of sleep. For people who experience sleep apnea or heavy snoring, they usually cannot get into the deep sleep delta brain wave state (0.5–4.0 Hz), which is important for our restoration and rejuvenation. Therefore they feel fatigued and tired during the day, even after eight hours of sleep.

The best indication to see whether you have sleep issues is to assess your state of mind, your body, and your emotions during the day. If you feel tired, experience mind fog, have loss of short-term memory, and feel irritated and impatient during the day, it is most likely a direct result of lack of good sleep. Sometimes we are so used to this way of living life that we do not see it as a real problem, and over time it becomes a chronic situation, leading to major illnesses and dysfunctions.

It is also important to give your digestive system a rest on a regular basis by fasting. There are many types and durations of fasts, but twenty-four-hour and thirty-six-hour food fasts are popular ways to maintain health and vigor. Fasting leverages the self-healing properties of the human body. Radical health improvements occur when the digestive system is given rest, and the organs get ample time to repair and heal themselves. A regular practice of fasting can improve mental clarity, increase physical and mental vigor, and remove toxins from your system. Fasting is also one of the most recognized techniques in religious and spiritual practices to get mental coherence and inner clarity. Like all the other habits, fasting gets easier with practice.

We have talked about the multitude of the benefits of meditation. Having a daily meditation practice acts like a detox for the mind, helps reduce mind noise, and increases thought coherence and clarity. In deep states of meditation, your brain waves are lowered to theta waves (4–8 Hz), where you can have access to the realm of the subconscious mind. This is where you can plant the seeds of your intention and nurture them through visualization, focused attention, and action in order to bear fruits and allow your vision to manifest itself.

It is also critical to schedule three-day to five-day retreats every six to twelve months, where you consciously step out of your daily routine to reflect and contemplate on your life's priorities and values. These retreats help you assess the alignment of your actions with your intentions and your heart's desires. It is best to pick a destination spot that is away from distractions, in or close proximity to nature. Natural settings of oceans, mountains, forests, or deserts have a unique effect on opening our hearts and minds to insights and to our internal wisdom. It is important for each of us to find our own unique power spots where we can recharge ourselves on a regular basis.

MEANING

> *"He who has a why to live can bear with almost any how." —Nietzsche*

As we evolve and raise our levels of consciousness, we gradually grow out of our will to pleasure and will to power, and we step into our will to meaning and service. What we need is not a tensionless state, but rather striving, and sometimes even struggling, for some goal worthy of ourselves—a goal that transcends beyond our egoic selves. Leading a life of meaning and purpose is a path that is unique to each of us; it is our hero's journey. Our vision of this path will only become clear when we look into our own hearts. In a sense, the purpose of life is to live a life of purpose. And when we align our actions toward that purpose, our life becomes a magnificent powerhouse of joy, impact and abundance.

> *"True happiness is not attained through self-gratification, but through fidelity to a worthy purpose." —Helen Keller*

What do you stand for in your life? When do you feel most alive? What matters to you most? What legacy do you want to leave behind? Ask yourself these questions periodically and see whether your actions are in integrity and in alignment with your purpose. If you don't yet have a clear picture of your purpose, get into action. Experiment, move in a direction (any direction), and course correct as you go along. Keep the intention of discovering your purpose in your mind, and put yourself to test. Keep an open mind and know that there are no wrong ways, only learnings and course adjusting. Over time, there comes a time when you feel the resonance toward some things. You feel the pull like a magnet drawing you closer to your deep-seated purpose. When you get inspired to action, answer the call courageously.

PRACTICE: OPTIMUM HEALTH

The practices in this section are intended to bring it all together and help you create a holistic and integrative approach to optimum health. This is your opportunity to design a lifestyle that is the foundation upon which to build joy, impact, and abundance.

Self-assessment

What areas of your life need more attention? Rate yourself in the following areas from scale of one to ten, where one needs the most attention.

- Physical activity
- Nutrition
- Mental
- Emotional
- Rest
- Meaning

Optimize Yourself

For each of the areas with a low rating, pick a few goals and practices from the list below that you resonate with, or add your own. Make a commitment to integrate them into your life.

Physical Activity

- Baseline of thirty to sixty minutes' physical activity on a daily basis

- Aerobics exercises
- Strength-building exercises
- Stretch movement exercises
- Balance-training exercises
- [Add your own]

Nutrition

- Eat mostly whole foods and plant-based diet, while minimizing the consumption of refined foods, added salt, and added fat. Use the table on page 110 to help you with the food selection.
- Drink six to eight glasses of clean water per day.
- Choose naturally grown organic foods and fresh, locally grown fruits and vegetables.
- [Add your own]

Mental

- Catch yourself having ANTs (Automatic Negative Thoughts), or limiting beliefs, and then put them up for investigation to question their truth. Consciously shift your thoughts to a more positive and empowering state.
- Choose a mental workout practice. Try new things, learn new skills, and challenge yourself and your habits in order to expand your horizons.
- [Add your own]

Emotional

- Make a conscious effort to connect with people you meet at a deeper level. Exercise vulnerability, ask penetrating questions, and invite honest and intimate conversations.
- Create or join a community of people with which you feel a sense of support and belonging. This could be people from your church or your spiritual practice. Seek a group of like-minded people with common values and interests.
- [Add your own]

Rejuvenation

- Get into the practice of daily meditation for at least thirty minutes.
- Do a water-based fast for twenty-four to thirty-six hours on a weekly basis.
- Schedule a three-day to five-day personal retreat over the next six to twelve months.
- Improve the quality of your sleep. Avoid the use of electronics and vigorous physical or mental activities for at least one to two hours before sleep.
- [Add your own]

Meaning

- What is your why? What do you stand for in your life?
- When do you feel most alive? What matters to you most?
- What legacy do you want to leave behind?
- [Add your own]

Tools and Resources

Self-assessment

To get a view of where you stand in terms of health across multiple dimensions, it is good to take a whole-health self-assessment and pay attention to areas with a low score. For a complimentary assessment, go to http://nader.app.selfoptima.com.

Fasting

Fasting is a natural detoxification therapy that has been used for thousands of years to improve health and vitality. In some cases, it helps treat and even cure many ailments. For more information and to explore what works best for you, go to http://www.allaboutfasting.com.

Genomics

DNA testing can help you understand your health risks, reveal how your body responds to the world around you, and it can lead to a personalized plan for a healthier lifestyle. Some examples are https://www.pathway.com and https://www.23andme.com.

Mental workout

There are several organizations that have developed online tools and games to improve your mental performance. Among them are http://www.mentalworkout.com and https://www.lumosity.com.

Quantified Self

Quantified Self Movement which began in 2007 tries to incorporate technology into data acquisition and analysis on different aspects of a person's daily life. These may include exercise and movements, food and nutrition intake, quality of air, mood shifts, quality and quantity of sleep, physical and mental performance, etc. The promise is self-knowledge through self-tracking utilizing technology. Since then, many wearable devices and gadgets have been introduced to market to help raise awareness. For more information check out http://quantifiedself.com/

FINAL WORDS

Turn passion into action. Act from love and compassion. Manifest with wisdom. Know that the path to freedom starts with opening to and recognizing your own true self. It is finding your own way of being and feeling at home with it. It is honoring and living in alignment with your heart's desires. The interplay between joy, impact, and abundance is not linear and sequential. It is a dynamic and regenerative process. When you are in joy, your creative genius awakens, and you want to make an impact. When you make an impact, abundance comes to you. When you are in abundance, you are in a position of making a deeper impact. When you make a worthy impact, you create joy for yourself and for the people around you. The spiral continuum of regeneration and co-creation continues. The starting point of the spiral is your essence, your seed; the other end of it is pointing to freedom, to infinity. Each spiral is the unfolding signature of the unique you. You cannot copy, imitate, or follow a path that has already been travelled by another. You can honor and learn from others' experiences, and you can listen to guides and helpers that you meet on your way, but ultimately you have to find and walk on your own path.

"Throw away my book; do not let it satisfy you. Do not think your truth can be found by anyone else; be

ashamed of nothing more than that. Throw away my book; say to yourself that it is only one of the thousand possible postures in life. Look for your own. Do not do what someone else could do as well as you. Do not say, do not write what someone else could say, could write as well as you. Care for nothing in yourself but what you feel exists nowhere else, and out of yourself create, impatiently or patiently, ah! The most irreplaceable of beings." —Andre Gide

References

Aimone, Steven. *Expressive Drawing: A Practical Guide to Freeing the Artist Within*. Lark Crafts, 2009.

Alvarez, Francisco. "Why, Scientifically, You Should Think with Your Heart, Not Your Brain," *Elite Daily* (Feb 2015).

Assagioli, Roberto. *Psychosynthesis: A Collection of Basic Writings*. Synthesis Center, 2000.

Berceli, David MD., *Trauma Releasing Exercises*. BookSurge Publishing, 2005.

Brazier, Brendan. *The Thrive Diet*. Penguin, 2007.

Campbell, T. Colin, and Thomas M. Campbell. *The China Study*. Ben Bella Books, 2006.

Chandler, Steve, Time Warrior. Maurice Bassett, 2011.

Dispenza, Joe. *Breaking the Habit of Being Yourself*. Hay House, 2013.

Dispenza, Joe. *You Are the Placibo: Making Your Mind Matter.* Hay House, 2015.

Dow, Mike. *Supercharge Your Brain: Simple Ways to Create Optimal Brain Health.* Jenkins Group, 2017.

Evans, Mike. "*23* 1/2 Hour: What Is the Single Best Thing We Can Do for Our Health." https://ed.ted.com/featured/Mot8KdLT.

Frankl, Victor E.. *Man's Search for Meaning.* Beacon Press, 2006.

Fuhrman, Joel. *Eat to Live.* Little Brown & Company, 2011.

Fuhrman, Joel. *Super Immunity.* HarperOne, 2013.

Hyman, Mark. *The UltraMind Solution.* Scribner, 2010.

Junger, Alejandro. *Clean.* HarperOne, 2012.

Kataria, Maden., *Laughter Yoga: Daily laughter practices for health and happiness.* Ebury Press, 2018.

Lesley Lyle. *Laugh Your Way to Happiness: The Science of Laughter for Total Well-Being.* Watkins Publishing, 2014.

Nennedy, David Daniel. *Feng Shui for Dummies.* For Dummies, 2010.

Pelletier, Kenneth R. *The New Medicine.* DK, 2009.

Radin, Dean. *Entangled Minds: Extrasensory Experiences in a Quantum Reality.* Paraview Pocket Books, 2006.

Rankin, Lissa MD., *Mind Over Medicine: Scientific proof that you can heal yourself.* Hay House Inc. 2014.

Ray, Michael. *The Highest Goal.* Berrett-Koehler Publishers, 2005.

Rollin McCraty Ph.D., *Science of the Heart, Volume 2: Exploring the Role of the Heart in Human Performance.* HeartMath, 2015.

Rosenthal, Joshua. *Integrative Nutrition.* Integrative Nutrition Publishing, 2014.

Vithoulkas, George. *The Science of Homeopathy.* Grove Weidenfeld, 1980.

ABOUT THE AUTHOR

Nader Vasseghi is an entrepreneur, CEO and executive coach based in Silicon Valley, California. He is the founder of Cnergist Inc., an executive coaching firm, committed to transforming and elevating the lives of business leaders and high achievers. He models and teaches the principles of his book to help his clients live from their essence and lead a life of Joy, Impact and Abundance. He conducts workshops, leads mastermind groups, and offers leadership training and executive coaching programs at corporate and individual levels. He is an advisor and board member of several private and public companies.

He is also the founder of SelfOptima Inc. a web based platform to empower people on their journey to optimal health. He was the founder and CEO of AuroraNetics which was acquired by Cisco where he went on to lead a business unit. He served as an adjunct professor at Palo Alto University, Business Psychology program.

He is a Vistage chair, speaker, workshop leader, certified hypnotherapist and energy medicine practitioner. He uses an integrated approach of ancient wisdom and modern science to help his clients overcome their limitations and live out their highest vision. His mission is to be the messenger of love, beauty and strength. He enjoys composing music, painting and gardening in his spare time. To learn more about him and his work, you can reach him at www. cnergist.com or at www.nadervasseghi.com